THE BIG BOOK
OF HATCH CHILE

KELLEY CLEARY COFFEEN

THE BIG BOOK
OF HATCH CHILE

180 GREAT RECIPES FEATURING THE WORLD'S FAVORITE CHILE PEPPER

UNIVERSITY OF NEW MEXICO PRESS ▲ ALBUQUERQUE

ISBN 978-0-8263-6543-9 (paper)
ISBN 978-0-8263-6544-6 (electronic)

Library of Congress Control Number: 2023942005

Founded in 1889, the University of New Mexico sits on the traditional homelands of the Pueblo of Sandia. The original peoples of New Mexico—Pueblo, Navajo, and Apache—since time immemorial have deep connections to the land and have made significant contributions to the broader community statewide. We honor the land itself and those who remain stewards of this land throughout the generations and also acknowledge our committed relationship to Indigenous peoples. We gratefully recognize our history.

Cover photograph by Marty Snortum Studio
Title page photograph by Dru Shiflett
Interior photographs by Kelley Cleary Coffeen
Designed by Felicia Cedillos
Composed in Alegreya

To Lisa Ekus, my agent and friend, your expertise, vision and guidance have taken me places I could not have imagined. Your willingness to explore new talent is magical. I am forever grateful you took a chance on me.

CONTENTS

PREFACE

Heading up to Hatch, the back way, along Highway 185. Wandering through the serene pecan orchards, passing small farms and old homesteads before crossing the Rio Grande River. Leisurely driving along in anticipation for the first day of the Hatch Chile Festival . . . the smell of roasting chile in the air, sweet music, and smiling faces all around. A burlap bag of fresh-picked Hatch green chile ready to roast, a cold beer, and a "World Famous" green chile cheeseburger await. It's gonna be a good day in Hatch.

ACKNOWLEDGMENTS

This culinary adventure started thirty years ago when I had my first taste of and opportunity to cook with Hatch chile. After cooking intensely with Hatch chile and visiting the village more frequently, I can honestly say it is true love. I love visiting Hatch, which is only forty miles up the road. It's quaint, friendly, and the landscape of farmland is so inviting. I have found the people who live in Hatch to be kind and interesting. They enjoy their community and are genuinely happy: happy to share local information, happy to guide you to the hot spots, and happy to talk chile. What an experience. God bless Hatch, New Mexico!

I have been testing, writing, and tasting recipes for over twenty-five years in southern New Mexico, all the while cooking with New Mexico chile: red, green, fresh, dried, ground powders, and spice mixes. Focusing on Hatch chile has given me a new appreciation for the producers' detailed attention to seed varieties, farming techniques, and processing. The farmers and processors have taken the Hatch chile "farm to table" experience to the next level, and we all benefit from that.

First, to my readers, thank you for cooking along with me through the years. It has been an adventure, and I appreciate you. To Jeff Witte, the secretary of agriculture for New Mexico and his team, Anthony Parra, Jason New, and Juan Sanchez, a big thank you for your support and resources. Thank you, Rachel Schneider and Keith Whelpley, owners of Ol' Gringo Chile Company; Art Alba and Vickie and Chuck Watkins of Village Market; Jo Lylte and her team at Hatch Chile Express; the Morrow Family;

the Shiflett Family; Teako and Josie Nunn, owners of Sparky's Burgers, Barbeque, and Espresso; Preston Michell, owner of the Hatch Chile Store; and Randy McMillan, owner of the Fresh Chile Company. To Don and Ellie Hackey, thank you for the conversations about the history of and life in the Hatch Valley.

A special thanks to the Chile Pepper Institute at New Mexico State University, Lisa Franzoy and the staff at the Hatch Library, and the staff at the New Mexico State University Library in Special Collections.

As always, my family encourages and cheers me on, over and over again. Thank you for letting me create family time around chile tastings and photo shoots! To my husband, Roger . . . it was a jam-packed year full of cooking, tasting, photo shoots, and Hatch Valley adventures. Thank you! A special thanks to my good friend and recipe tester, Maria Gallegos Pacheco, your cooking expertise is a gift. To Leslie and Dino Cervantes, Cynthia and Claiborne Gallagher, Chris and Joanne Cleary, Sandy and Bruce Weber, and Kathy and Buddy Achen, many thanks for the tastings, chile chats, and feedback.

To the rest of my family and friends: I made it through another joyful year of cooking and writing, with your support . . . Frosty Chile Ritas soon!

This book would not have been possible without the hard work and guidance of Lisa and Sally Ekus, my literary agents, of the Ekus Group. Thank you so much for cultivating the perfect project and always elevating the experience. To Stephen Hull, director of UNM Press, thank you for believing in the special project and pushing me to a new level of writing and photography. Many thanks to James Ayers, Min Marcus, and Irina du Quenoy, who walked me through the editing process with ease, and to Felicia Cedillos for creating such an incredibly beautiful book. A special thank you to Marty Snortum for the perfect cover photo.

Finally, thank you to the entire agricultural community. From the chile researchers, educators, suppliers, processors, and growers to the workers in the fields: your hard work and daily dedication give us this beautiful chile crop and so much more. I appreciate you.

INTRODUCTION

HATCH CHILE MAC, HATCH CHRISTMAS ENCHILADAS, Hatch Chile
Caramel Ice Cream Shake, Hatch Chile Dirty Martini, and don't forget
the famous Hatch Green Chile Cheeseburger. Sound intriguing? You have
heard of Hatch chile, right? Hatch chile is known around the world. The
New York Times, *LA Times*, the Food Network, *Southern Living Magazine*,
and many other outlets have reported on our beloved Hatch chile. It has a
strong following among celebrity chefs, politicians, actors, and restaura-
teurs, but more importantly, it is beloved by people just like you and me.

I call it "Heavenly Hatch." It's a beautiful valley along the Rio Grande
in southern New Mexico, a farming community with a small village nestled in the middle, with a population around seventeen hundred. The tiny
village of Hatch is known as the Chile Capital of the World.[1]

This is no surprise to me as a New Mexican, and it warrants a trip or
two every month to my local grocer or farmers market to get my chile fix.
During the late summer harvest, I often take the beautiful drive forty
miles up the road from my home in Las Cruces, New Mexico, to get my
chile, freshly picked and roasted for an authentic experience. I have a
confession: I eat chile nearly every day—some days red, some days green,
some days both. During the harvest season the unforgettable scent of
roasting chiles hangs in the air across the Hatch Valley. It is addicting.

Hatch, New Mexico, boasts neighbors like Virgin Galactic and the
Spaceport right up the road, as well as Sparky's Burgers, Barbeque, and
Espresso, a James Beard award nominee. The Chile Pepper Institute, at

New Mexico State University (just down the hall from my office), is an international horticultural institute devoted to educating the world about chile peppers. This is the heart of chile country. Every Labor Day weekend brings the Hatch Chile Festival: two days of celebrating Hatch chile via parades, chile-eating contests, dancing, chile tasting, and carnivals. Chile lovers from around the country (over thirty thousand in 2021) come to celebrate Hatch chile. It has been happening since the 1970s and gets better every year.

If you pull off I-25 going north or south at the Hatch exit, you'll find chile shops with chile ristras hanging out front and "Open" signs asking for your business. The line outside of Sparky's Burgers, Barbeque, and Espresso and the smell of the grill tells you it's time for a World-Famous Green Chile Cheeseburger, their bestselling burger. Turning west on Hall Street leads to more chile shops filled with salsas, ristras, and beautiful tin yard ornaments galore. You may want to stop in at the Village Market, where you can grab a green chile chicken burrito or the Friday Special, which is usually freshly made green or red chile enchiladas.

I have lived in chile country for the past thirty years, creating and writing over fifteen hundred Mexican, Tex Mex, Southwest, and border-style recipes. So, I appreciate a good culinary experience, especially created with Hatch chile—something I can always find in the village. So, the question is, When are you coming to Hatch?

Hatch

Established in 1880 between the Santa Fe Railroad and the Rio Grande River, the town was originally named Santa Barbara (in 1851). Its name was changed a few years later to honor General E. Hatch, the commander of nearby Fort Thorn. Hundreds of folks came to homestead the land in the valley. Many of today's families are descendants of immigrants from Europe and early Spanish settlers.[2]

They came because of the proximity of this valley to the river. The soil, the hot summer days, and the cool nights create the perfect environment to grow a high-quality chile with thick texture, good flavor, and a high heat level. Settlers in the Hatch Valley started growing chile in the early

1900s. Through the years, this agricultural community has focused on improving and growing Hatch chile; however, farmers also grow onions, lettuce, cabbage, sweet potatoes, watermelon, pecans, wheat, and cotton.

Hatch Chile

Hatch chile peppers are versatile and full of flavor. They manifest different levels of heat and have the ability to elevate the flavor of almost any culinary combination. These long, green chile peppers, grown for decades in the Hatch Valley by legendary farming families, are the signature crop of New Mexico. In the 1920s Fabian Garcia, a pioneer horticulturist from Mexico, began to breed and standardize green chile peppers at the New Mexico Agricultural College (now known as New Mexico State University). The "hot" varieties of Hatch chile were enjoyed regionally; however, sales of chile outside the region were limited due to the high heat levels. Over the next few decades, horticulturists working with local farmers were able to develop seed varieties that produced chile with lower levels of heat, creating the opportunity for growers to sell chiles to consumers not as accustomed to heat throughout the United States and eventually around the world.

Hatch chile enjoys a pure, crisp earthy flavor and dense texture. Thousands of acres are harvested annually in late summer, producing tons of fresh green chile.[3] A portion of this chile is sold fresh to roadside stands, individuals, and grocery stores across the country, where it is roasted for immediate consumption or stored in home freezers for the winter. The remaining portion is processed for the food manufacturing market by many local processors.

Processed chile includes dehydrated, frozen, freeze-dried, canned, and pickled varieties. Dehydrated chile is used as a component in spice mixes for flavorings in soups, sauces, dips, and in processed foods for the food-service industry. Wet-processed chile is used for canned, frozen, and pickled products utilized in sauces and prepared meals and snacks, sold directly to retailers and food-service sectors.

Through the years, chile from the Hatch Valley became more and more popular through agricultural innovation, marketing partnerships, and the establishment of the Hatch Chile Festival. Eventually, Hatch Valley growers pursued trademark certification protecting their crop's name and reputation to ensure their customers were buying authentic, Hatch-grown green and red chile.[4]

Today, the annual harvest at the end of summer brings an abundance of chile in a short amount of time, creating a frenzy among locals and Hatch chile fans from around the country. These long, green chiles offer a fresh, spicy flavor that is magically balanced: not too hot or too mild. Chile lovers just can't get enough of them, buying twenty-five to forty-pound bags of freshly harvested chile to roast and freeze for the winter. And that's just the beginning! Every year a portion of the chile is left to dry on the vine until September. These chiles turn a deep red color and offer a smoky, earthy red chile flavor when harvested. Hatch red chile makes the perfect red sauce for enchiladas, stews, soups, sauces for meats, tamales, tacos, and burritos. And all varieties of Hatch chile can be stuffed, broiled, liquefied, sautéed, baked, and roasted.

Chile Tasting

HEAT AND VARIETIES

Chile is measured in Scoville heat units (SHU). This is a measurement of the number of times capsaicin needs to be diluted by sugar water. Complicated? Maybe a little. Capsaicin is an irritant that produces a sensation of burning to our skin. So just remember this: the higher the Scoville number the hotter the chile. Given these varying levels of heat, I sometimes call for "hot" Hatch chile in recipes that need that extra heat flavor for the best results.

There are many varieties of chile grown in the Hatch Valley, with new varieties being developed continually. Here are a few, along with their heat levels:

> NuMex 6–4: 1,000 to 1,500 SHU
> NuMex Heritage 6–4: 3,000 to 5,000 SHU
> NuMex Big Jim: 2,500 to 3,000 SHU
> NuMex Sandia: 5,000 to 7,000, SHU

NuMex R Naky: 500 to 1,000 SHU
Barker Extra Hot: 15,000 to 30,000 SHU
Big Jim: 500 to 3,500 SHU
NuMex Heritage Big Jim: 9,000 SHU

Benefits

The benefits of green and red chile are not only culinary but also health related. Studies show that natural chile has nutrients that act as metabolism boosters and may help prevent muscular degeneration and inflammation. Each chile is loaded with immuno-protective vitamin C and vitamin E. Additionally, consumption of chile is known to help maintain the health of skin, cartilage, teeth, bone, and blood vessels, protecting the immune system.[5] Eating well is a priority for myself and my readers. We enjoy flavorful food that supports good health. Locally, we often say, "Red and green chile will cure what ails you!" That's why the recipes presented in this book leverage both the health benefits of Hatch chile and their exceptional flavors.

Notably, I offer exceptional flavor combinations, like my favorite Chile Lemon Drop Martini or a Frosty Chile Rita along with alcohol-free refreshers like Chile Lemonitas and Spicy Sweet Tea. I often pair these with my chile-laced appetizers, such as Hatch Chile Chicken Lettuce Wraps or Prosciutto and Chile Bruschetta. These recipes are easy to whip up and can be prepared ahead of time.

Hatch chile has a way of accenting and elevating many different foods. My collection of homemade salsa, relish, and sauces is bursting with flavor and remarkably inexpensive to make. I love a culinary surprise, and that is what you get when you add these condiments to everything from grilled meats to roasted veggies and rice. Spread a bit of Orange Chile Glaze over the top of a roasted turkey breast or a slice of baked ham. Drizzle some Hatch Vinaigrette over a crisp green salad or change up your grilled chicken with a spoonful of Hatch Bacon Jam. The best news is most of these salsas and sauces can be placed in a bowl and simply served with warm tortillas or bagel chips.

I offer amazing "one pot" soups and stews that have become my "go-to" for simple meals year-round. They are flavorful and filling, rich and creamy, or light and brothy. Try my Bacon and Potato Green Chile Chowder or a lighter Albondigas Sopa served with a crusty loaf of bread for a perfect dinner.

Now let's talk about my favorite "handhelds" . . . burgers, sandwiches, and flatbreads! I offer you a collection of recipes that are easy to make and great to share with friends and family.

The amazing Hatch Green Chile Cheeseburger is iconic, a true New Mexico classic. I can eat and enjoy this burger anytime. But just as impressive are my Hatch Chile Philly, Hatch Pastrami Sandwich, and Hatch Garden-Fresh Flatbreads, all packed with chile flavor. Now, large or small, gatherings often call for impressive entrées. My adventurous chile cooking has led me to create crowd-pleasers like Green Chile Chicken Alfredo, Red Chile Salmon, and Chile Filet Mignon. My plant-based dishes, such as the Chile Relleno Black Bean Bake, will impress and satisfy.

Traditional Mexican fare is the cornerstone of our cooking in this region, so I have included a variety of Mexican favorites, such as Grilled Carne Asada Tacos and our smothered New Mexico Christmas (red and green) Burritos. I offer a variety of burrito, taco, and enchilada fillings so you can create your own customized favorites.

My family knows that I could eat breakfast burritos and breakfast taquitos every day. Starting the day with chile is just how we live around here. Enjoy my savory Green Chile Gravy, which is rich and creamy and so delicious on fresh baked biscuits or fluffy scrambled eggs. My crispy Breakfast Rolled Tacos stuffed with breakfast sausage and Hatch chile are good and savory. On a sweeter note, indulge in my Spicy Sweet Cinnamon Rolls for a luscious companion to your morning coffee.

Speaking of sweets, through my cooking experience I have found that the red and green chile flavors pair nicely with fruits, chocolate, and nuts. The chile flavor and heat lend themselves to sweets in unique and subtle ways. So I offer a few special desserts, such as my Mexican Chocolate Pecan Pie and Chile Apple Chimichangas. And my Spicy Bananas Flambé laced with red chile is truly unforgettable!

As you see, this cookbook is full of recipes that call for fresh Hatch chile, dried Hatch chile, ground Hatch chile powders, prepared Hatch chile sauces, and spice mixes. To make these ingredients more accessible, I have included information on food retailers that will ship Hatch chile products directly to you. Check out my Hatch Chile Marketplace (175) and order what you need.

So, friends and chile lovers, as you anticipate the annual late-summer harvest of fresh green chile, enjoy this recipe collection and use it to plan each curated chile dish all year long! And if you get a chance to visit Hatch, New Mexico, take it! I might just see you there.

Notes

1. Hatch Valley Friends of the Library, *History of the Hatch Valley* (Hatch, NM: Hatch Valley Friends of the Library, 1989).

2. Hatch Valley Friends of the Library, *History of the Hatch Valley*.

3. United States Department of Agriculture, *2021 New Mexico Chile Production*, https://www.nass.usda.gov/Statistics_by_State/New_Mexico/Publications/Special_Interest_Reports/NM-2021-Chile-Production.pdf.

4. Samantha Lewis, "Hatch Green Chile Now Protected by Certification Label," CBS *Channel 4 News*, July 5, 2016, https://cbs4local.com/news/local/hatch-green-chile-now-protected-by-certification-label.

5. I. Guzman, "The Chile Pepper: It's Nutritious and Delicious!" presentation at the Annual New Mexico Chile Conference, Las Cruces, New Mexico, 2017.

CHILE FACTS

- Chile peppers are fruits, not vegetables.
- One fresh green chile pod has as much vitamin C as six oranges.
- One teaspoon of dried red chile powder has the daily requirements of vitamin A.
- Hot chile peppers burn calories by triggering a thermodynamic burn, which speeds up the metabolism.
- Green and red chile are very high in dietary fiber.
- Oleoresin, the color extracted from very red chile pepper pods, is used in everything from lipstick to processed meats.
- The average American eats about sixteen pounds of chile peppers per year.
- The best way to cut the heat is to drink or eat a dairy product. Dairy has a protein called casein that breaks the binding site of your skin receptors and the capsaicin molecule.

Note
Information provided by the Chile Pepper Institute, New Mexico State University, 2019.

ROASTING CHILES

COME AUGUST THE AROMA IS IN the air . . .

You can feel the excitement up and down the valley as people stand outside the markets while metal drums of green chile rotate slowly over open flames. In restaurants across New Mexico, special chile dishes appear on the menu and tailgate and picnic fare is focused on Hatch green chile. Everyone is roasting and eating chile.

Fresh picked chile is roasted over high heat in order to blister the tough outer skin so it can be peeled. Once the skin is removed, it is ready for cooking or eating. I have included steps in this process that create the best outcome for roasted chile, whether you have it roasted at the market or roast it at home. Let's explore both.

(*opposite page*) Hatch fresh green chile getting flame roasted while rotating in roaster

(*left*) Fresh Hatch green chile, flame roasted and cooled down with a water process that removes the skin

It is hard for some people to understand why Hatch chile lovers buy twenty-five-pound boxes (or more!) of chile during harvest season. I have found over the years that no matter how much chile I buy for the year and put in the freezer, it is usually gone by the next year's harvest.

But we need our chile. So, let's do this!

Essential materials: Quart- and gallon-sized resealable bags, black permanent marker, ice chest (for transporting), 2 bags of ice (to cool after roasting).

The key to storing Hatch chile is being prepared, so there are few things you have to do in order to bring your fresh roasted chile home. I often place smaller chiles in quart-sized bags (4 to 6 chiles). I use these for recipes that call for chopped or minced chile. I place larger chiles in gallon-sized bags (6 to 8 chiles) together. I use these for chile relleno recipes or when cooking for a crowd.

If you are getting it roasted in bulk (meaning more than ten pounds) on site, bring an ice chest and a couple of bags of ice. Select your burlap bag or box of Hatch green chile. Pay and give it to the chile handler and watch them roast. It is a treat—from fresh, plump raw chile to a beautiful, green, almost velvety looking roasted chile in a matter of minutes.

If you are lucky enough to get your roast done in Hatch or nearby, chile handlers will most likely use the water-spray method, where they shoot water into the turning cage, which, miraculously, takes most of the charred skin off. However, other places just roast the chile, so you may have charred skin to remove once you get home.

Once the chile is done roasting, the chile handler will drop it into a large plastic bag for you. Now, it is still pretty hot. Pour a bag of ice over the chile and move it around a bit. Then put the chile (now in the plastic bag with the ice over it) in your ice chest and pour the second bag of ice over the top of the chile for the ride home. Cooling the chile down quickly keeps good color and prevents the chile from breaking down from the heat.

Fresh-roasted Hatch green chile cooled with ice to preserve color and texture

Once I am in my kitchen, I rinse my chile, gently taking off any charred skin in a sink filled with water. I dry the chile on paper towels and then start bagging it, laying the chile horizontally in each bag to put in the freezer and tasting along the way, of course. Again, I often place 6 or 10 chiles in individual resealable plastic bags (quart-sized for smaller chile, gallon-sized for larger chile). I label my chile "chopped," "rellenos," or whatever helps me pull out the right chile for cooking throughout the year. Now, place a few bags in the refrigerator so you can get your chile fix immediately and stack the rest in the freezer. Don't forget to wash your hands thoroughly after handling chiles. You can wear kitchen gloves (latex or latex free) to protect your hands during this process. If you do get chile in your eye, mouth, or nose, rinse thoroughly with water. It will burn for a bit but should go away within minutes.

Some chile lovers like to roast their own chile. This is great for small quantities as well. You can roast at home several different ways: on the grill, on the stove top (if you have a gas range), or broiled in the oven.

Outdoor Gas Grill

Preheat an outdoor grill to medium-high heat. Place fresh chiles on grill grate. Cook, turning often with tongs, as the skin of the chile blisters. When each chile is lightly charred and blistered, remove from heat. Immediately place chiles in a plastic bag or an airtight container and close tightly. Let chiles cool to room temperature. If using immediately, peel off

Broiling fresh green chiles in the oven is quick and easy.

charred skin and remove stems and seeds. Tear into strips or chop as needed according to the recipe. If not, place 6 or 10 chiles in individual resealable plastic bags. Refrigerate chile for up to 3 days or freeze for up to 12 months. Wash your hands thoroughly after handling chiles.

Oven Roasted

Preheat an oven broiler. Place fresh chiles on a baking sheet and place 2 to 3 inches away from heat under the broiler. Broil, turning often with tongs, until the skin surfaces are lightly charred and blistered. Immediately place chiles in a plastic bag or an airtight container and close tightly. Let chiles cool to room temperature. If using immediately, peel off charred skin and remove stems and seeds. Tear into strips or chop as needed according to the recipe. If not, place 6 or 10 chiles in individual resealable plastic bags (quart-sized for 6, gallon-sized for 10). Refrigerate chile for up to 3 days or freeze for up to 12 months. Wash your hands thoroughly after handling chiles.

Gas Stove Top

Arrange fresh chiles on a comal or small metal grate for a gas range. Roast over medium-high flame, turning often with tongs, until surfaces of skin are lightly charred and blistered. Immediately place chiles in a plastic bag or an airtight container and close tightly. Let chiles cool to room temperature. If using immediately, peel off charred skin and remove stems and seeds. Tear into strips or chop as needed according to the recipe. If not,

Roasting individual chiles on a stove top using a comal, iron skillet, or small metal grate is easy and efficient.

place 6 or 10 chiles in individual resealable plastic bags (quart-sized for 6, gallon-sized for 10). Refrigerate chile for up to 3 days or freeze for up to 12 months. Wash your hands thoroughly after handling chiles.

1 COCKTAILS AND BEVERAGES

HATCH IS A FUN, FESTIVE, AND welcoming community. As people come and go, visit, shop, and dine they enjoy unique landmarks and local art, all with a backdrop of brightly colored signage, mostly about chile. In this small village, residential neighborhoods intertwine with the business district and educational community, everyone working together.

In that spirit, I have curated a collection of fun, quirky, bold recipes for cocktails and alcohol-free sippers. Creating the perfect libation takes more than simply mixing ingredients. My focus is on looking at primary flavors and layering them with a nuance of citrus, ales, and sweetness, all with a twist of Hatch chile—a sometimes slight, other times burning essential for ultimate flavor.

You will want to try my Spicy Sweet Tea and indulge in a Chocolaty Chile Fizz or a Hatchelada: a local draft of Mexican lager with a scoop of fresh Hatch green chile and fresh lime juice. Create your favorite and enjoy.

1

(*opposite page*) Year-round reminder for the Hatch Chile Festival.

CHILE LEMONITAS

MAKES 6 SERVINGS

This is a refreshing reboot on good, old-fashioned lemonade. New Mexicans can't help but add chile to almost everything! It is a unique twist of fresh lemons and green chile. It's intriguing.

1 ¾ cup granulated sugar
8 cups tap or bottled water
1 to 1 ½ cups fresh lemon juice, about 8 to 10 lemons
¼ cup hot Hatch green chile roasted, peeled, and seeded
2 tbsp. water

1. In a large pitcher combine sugar, water, and lemon juice. Mix well until sugar is dissolved.

2. In a small food processer combine chile and 2 tbsp. water. Pulse until smooth, mixing until a paste is formed. Alternatively, you can do this by hand, muddling with a wooden spoon or muddler until smooth.

3. Add the chile paste to the lemonade, one tablespoon at a time, blending well. Taste frequently until you get the desired heat and flavor. Serve in a tall glass over ice.

SPICY SWEET TEA

MAKES 6 SERVINGS

Sweet tea has been an American classic since the late 1800s. Originally from the South, it has definitely found a home in the West. But there are so many flavors of teas, countless varieties and combinations in flavor. Adding a little heat takes this tea up another level, creating a memorable drink.

> 6 to 8 tea bags
> 4 cups boiling water
> 1 cup Hatch Simple Syrup (32)
> 4 cups water
> Cracked ice
> 2 lemons, sliced
> 1 handful fresh mint, rinsed

1. Steep tea bags in boiling water in a large sauce pan for 30 to 40 minutes.

2. Remove tea bags, add simple syrup, and stir well. Then add remaining water. Mix well, transfer to a pitcher, and chill.

3. Before serving, fill glasses with cracked ice, a lemon slice, and a sprig of mint. Fill with tea and serve immediately.

Variation:: For a sweeter version add granulated sugar when adding syrup, one tablespoon at a time until desired sweetness.

SPICY LIME SPRITZER

MAKES 6 SERVINGS

Such an easy sipper for an afternoon on the patio or brunch with friends!
Enjoy flavors of a hint of chile, lime, and mint in this cocktail. It is a fun
and festive nonalcoholic beverage.

> 6 oz. fresh lime juice (about 12 medium limes)
> 1 cup Hatch Simple Syrup (32)
> 1 qt. tonic water
> Cracked ice
> Fresh mint leaves

1. In a large pitcher, combine lime juice, syrup, and tonic water. Mix well.
2. Fill tall glasses with ¾ glass of cracked ice and lime mixture. Garnish
   with mint.

Variation:: For a sweeter version omit the lime juice and add 6 oz. of lime concentrate.

HATCH CHILE CARAMEL ICE CREAM SHAKE

MAKES 2 SERVINGS

Weekends, summertime, date nights, movie nights . . . milkshakes are special, an indulgence that we relish. It's fun to offer the unexpected sweet chile flavor wrapped in caramel and cream. It is a chile lover's delight anytime, for any reason. I add a bit of ice to this recipe for frothiness.

> 2 cups (about 4 scoops) premium vanilla ice cream
> ½ cup whole milk
> ½ cup cracked ice
> 1 tsp. Hatch red chile powder (Hatch Chile Marketplace, 175), divided
> ½ cup Sweet Caramel Chile Sauce (118)
> 1 cup whipped cream topping*
> ½ cup whole or chopped pecans
> 1 cup caramel coated popcorn (such as Cracker Jacks)

1. Chill 2 16-oz. glasses in the freezer for 30 minutes to an hour.

2. In a blender, combine ice cream, milk, ice, and ½ tsp. chile powder. Blend for 1 to 2 minutes. Place in refrigerator while preparing each glass.

3. Remove glasses from freezer. Drizzle caramel sauce around the inside of the rim, allowing it to drizzle down the inside of the glass. Repeat with second glass.

4. Quickly and gently, fill each glass with ice cream mixture. Drizzle each with 1 tbsp. of caramel sauce, allowing it to drizzle on the outside of the glass.

5. Top with whipped cream, sprinkle with pecans, remaining chile powder, and caramel popcorn. Serve immediately.

* You can make whipped cream from scratch, but I often use canned whipped topping for ease and presentation.

MINI WHITE CHOCOLATE RASPBERRY CHILE SHAKE

MAKES 4 SERVINGS

A little "mini" shake is tasty after dinner or even in the middle of the afternoon . . . right? Creamy vanilla ice cream is the perfect backdrop to the
sweet spicy accent in this raspberry sauce.

- 2 ½ cups (about 4 to 5 scoops) premium vanilla ice cream
- 1 ½ tbsp. white chocolate flavored syrup
- ¼ cup whole milk
- 4 tbsp. Hatch Chile Raspberry Sauce (119) or
    Quick Raspberry Sauce (120)
- Whipped cream topping*
- 3 to 4 fresh raspberries
- 1 tbsp. shaved white chocolate

1. Chill four 8-oz. glasses in the freezer for 30 minutes to an hour.

2. In a blender, blend together ice cream, syrup, and milk for 1 to 2 minutes, until just well blended.

3. Pour raspberry chile sauce evenly down the insides and in the bottom of
   each glass.

4. Slowly pour blended milkshake into each serving glass.

5. Garnish with whipped cream, raspberries, and shaved chocolate.

* You can make whipped cream from scratch, but I often use canned whipped topping for ease and presentation.

CHOCOLATY CHILE FIZZ

MAKES 1 SERVING

There is just something about an old-fashioned soda! Creamy but light, laced with tiny bubbles . . . A hint of chile flavor adds to the rich chocolate taste. Try this fun retro libation for a fizzy, creamy experience.

¼ cup cold whole milk
3 tbsp. chocolate syrup
1 tbsp. hot Hatch green chile, roasted, seeded, peeled, and muddled
1 scoop vanilla ice cream
1 scoop chocolate ice cream
4 to 6 oz. club soda or sparkling water
Whipped cream topping*
1 tbsp. shaved chocolate

1. Chill a 16-oz. glass in the freezer for 30 minutes to an hour.

2. Remove glass from freezer.

3. Pour milk into chilled glass. Add chocolate syrup and chile, stirring well with a spoon.

4. Add ice cream scoops. Pour club soda over ice cream slowly and watch as bubbles rise to the top of the glass.

5. Garnish with whipped topping or cream and shaved chocolate. Serve immediately.

* You can make whipped cream from scratch, but I often use dairy whipped topping for ease and presentation.

HATCH WHISKEY SMASH

MAKES 1 SERVING

Muddling is key in this pungent cocktail: a lot of the flavor comes from the lemon skin that infuses with the alcohol, chile, and fresh mint. My version of the traditional smash is like a mint julep but with a citrusy, chile twist.

1 medium lemon, cut in 3 wedges
4 mint leaves
2 oz. bourbon
1 oz. Hatch Simple Syrup (32)
Cracked ice
Mint sprig

1. In a shaker add lemon wedges and muddle well, 2 to 3 minutes.

2. Add mint leaves, bourbon, and syrup. Top with ice and shake until well blended.

3. Strain into a rocks glass half full of ice and garnish with mint sprig.

HATCH CHILE DIRTY MARTINI

MAKES 1 SERVING

Classic cocktails stay with us forever. Changing them up from time to time keeps life interesting. I created a chile brine for this martini that adds a depth of flavor. Cheers to the classics!

  2 oz. gin or vodka
  ½ oz. dry vermouth
  ½ oz. Hatch green chile brine*
  2 to 3 olives and chile for garnish

1. Pour liquor, vermouth, and brine into a mixing glass filled with ice and stir until well chilled.

2. Strain into a chilled martini glass and garnish with olives and chile.

* Hatch green chile brine: Combine ½ cup water; ¼ cup vinegar; 1 tsp. kosher salt; and 1 Hatch chile, roasted, peeled, seeded, and muddled, in a sealable jar. Let stand 8 hours or overnight.

HATCHELADA

The Michelada is a favorite cocktail in Mexico of citrus and ale—the phrase *mi chela helada* means "my ice-cold beer" in Spanish. This is a summertime favorite in this region. Red chile salt kisses the senses as fresh green chile mingles with fresh lime juice in this Mexican lager cocktail, a local favorite.

> 1 fresh lime, sliced lengthwise in quarters
> 2 tbsp. Hatch Red Chile Salt (122)
> Cracked ice
> 1 bottle (12 oz.) Icebox Mexican Lager*
> ¼ cup freshly squeezed lime
> 1 tbsp. Hatch green chile, roasted, peeled, seeded, and minced

1. Rub the rim of a lager or ale beer glass with a lime quarter and dip into the salt mixture.

2. Fill glass half full with cracked ice. Add lime juice. Slowly top with beer.

3. Garnish with minced green chile and lime slices and serve. Add remaining beer to the glass as needed.

Variation: For a sweet-savory salted rim, add 1 tsp. brown sugar to Hatch Red Chile Salt.

* Mexican Lager from the Icebox Brewery (located in Hatch, NM) is a light Mexican-style lager. There are a variety of Mexican beers on the market. They all vary in taste, so try them and find your favorites.

SANGRITA

MAKES 4 SERVINGS

History has it that this libation was created as a tequila chaser and has become a Mexican tradition. Sangrita means "little blood" in Spanish. It is a carefully crafted combination of flavors that enhance the taste of our coveted tequilas. Adding the heat of my Hatch Simple Syrup gives it even more flavor.

1 cup tomato juice
¼ cup freshly squeezed orange juice
¼ cup freshly squeezed lime juice
1 tbsp. Hatch Simple Syrup (32)
1 tsp. Worcestershire sauce
2 tsp. hot pepper sauce*
Tequila

1. In a small pitcher, combine tomato juice, orange juice, lime juice, syrup, and Worcestershire sauce and pepper sauce. Mix well.

2. Serve up in 2-oz. shot glasses and sip slowly after taking a shot of tequila.

Variation: For a more savory version, omit Hatch Simple Syrup and add 1 tbsp. Hatch green chile, roasted, peeled, seeded, and minced.

*Tabasco or Louisiana Hot Sauce

CHILE LEMON DROP MARTINI

SERVES 1

The tart sweet flavor of this martini is enhanced with an infusion of chile. The simple syrup is smooth and spicy, melting into the sweetness of this cocktail. Shaken and served exquisitely for your guests.

¼ cup superfine sugar
1 lemon wedge
2 oz. vodka
1 oz. Cointreau
1 oz. Hatch Simple Syrup (32)
2 oz. fresh lemon juice
1 fresh Hatch green chile sliced into a thin strip
lemon rind

1. Spread sugar across a small plate.

2. Moisten the rim of a chilled martini glass with lemon wedge. Dip the rim in the sugar and set aside.

3. In a shaker full of ice, add vodka, Cointreau, syrup, and lemon juice. Shake for 30 seconds until cold. Pour into martini glass and garnish with fresh chile slice and lemon rind.

HATCH NOSH BLOODY MARY

MAKES 4 TO 6 SERVINGS

This cocktail says, "Good morning! Relax and enjoy." I add red chile puree to intensify the tomato flavor in this traditional cocktail. It gives it an elevated, earthy chile taste. Garnish with charcutier-style tidbits to make this a delightful drink.

> 2 lemons
> 2 to 3 tbsp. Hatch Red Chile Salt (122)
> 1 qt. tomato juice
> ½ cup Hatch Red Chile Puree (117)*
> 12 oz. vodka**
> 2 tsp. Worcestershire sauce
> Pinch of pepper

1. Cut 1 lemon into quarters and zest 1 lemon. Set aside.

2. Rub the rim of each glass with a lemon quarter and dip into the salt mixture.

3. In a large pitcher, combine tomato juice, chile puree, vodka, Worcestershire sauce, pepper, and lemon zest. Mix well.

4. Place ice in glasses and top with tomato mixture. Add garnish and prepared skewers (see notes).

* You can also find store-bought Hatch red chile puree at your local market, or see the Hatch Chile Marketplace (175).

** If you are not a vodka fan, omit vodka and add tequila, creating a Bloody Maria!

To garnish, create skewers with any combination of the following: small chunks of cheese, grape tomatoes, chile or jalapeño-stuffed olives, slice of summer sausage, cooked chicken nuggets, radishes, lemon wedges, orange wedges, small dill pickle, or cooked shrimp.

Additional garnish: Add 1 tbsp. Hatch green chile (chopped), a splash of beer floating on top, a leafy celery stalk, or tall strips of crispy cooked bacon.

Preparing skewers: Thread cocktail skewer with 3 to 4 garnishes, stacking at one end of the skewer. Place the skewer across the top of the salt-rimmed glass or into the cocktail with the garnished end up. You can also thread a smaller garnish stick that lays across the top of the glass.

YOUNG GUNS HATCH CHILE

More than eighty years ago Joseph and Celestina Franzoy immigrated to the Hatch Valley from Austria and started growing chile. Since then, several generations of the Franzoys have grown chile in the Hatch Valley, including Chris and Tammy Franzoy, fourth-generation farmers. In 1992 they formed the Young Guns Hatch Chile Corporation to continue the farming tradition, and in 2008 they added the Hatch Chile Factory to create premium Hatch chile products with availability year-round. Together, they produce high-quality, safe, nutritional, all-natural green and red chile products.

Today their family ships salsas, sauces, and frozen red and green chile around the world. You can find Young Guns Hatch Chile products in sixteen states and in nine different grocery chains across the United States.

For additional information see the Hatch Chile Marketplace (175).

"We eat chile on everything! Especially in pasta, and with pinto beans, which are a family favorite. We also love our chile paired with Spam for family favorites like Spam Rellenos." —CHRIS FRANZOY

True Hatch chile pioneers, the Franzoy family.

18

SPICY ROCKS MARGARITA

MAKES 1 SERVING

Ahhhh the margarita . . . our pride and joy around the borderland. The classic margarita is citrusy and refreshing. The rosemary flavor on the salted rim adds a depth of flavor at the onset, but sipping on this smooth libation leaves a hint of chile flavor behind, which is unique and addicting.

> 3 fresh medium-sized limes
> Hatch Rosemary Salt (121)
> 1 tbsp. hot Hatch green chile, roasted, peeled, and seeded
> 2 oz. silver tequila
> 1½ oz. Cointreau
> Cracked ice

1. Slice 1 lime into 4 slices. Rub the rim of a margarita glass with lime and dust with rosemary salt. Shake off any excess salt. Set glass aside.

2. Zest and juice the remaining limes, producing about 2 oz. fresh juice.

3. In a shaker, add green chile and water and muddle until chile is smooth.

4. Pour in tequila, Cointreau, lime zest, lime juice, and ice. Shake well.

5. Gently strain into salt-dusted, ice-filled glass and garnish with lime slices on the rim and in the glass.

FROSTY CHILE RITAS

MAKES 4 TO 6 SERVINGS

What's one more unique margarita recipe to add to your collection? I love frozen margaritas from time to time. Summer in the Southwest begs for this refreshing cocktail. My Frosty Chile Ritas sizzle with chile flavor. It's a nice balance of sweet, spicy, and citrusy flavors.

> ½ cup margarita or kosher salt
> Sliced lime
> 6 to 7 oz. silver tequila
> 8 oz. fresh lime juice*
> 3 oz. Cointreau
> ¾ to 1 cup Hatch Simple Syrup (32)**
> Cracked ice
> Lime zest
> 1 fresh Hatch green chile, seeded and sliced (optional)***

1. Pour salt across a small saucer or flat surface.

2. Rub the rim of each glass with a slice of lime. Dip in salt and place in freezer.

3. In blender add tequila, lime juice, Cointreau, and syrup.

4. Add ice and blend until slushy, 1 to 2 minutes. Add more ice, if desired. Pour into glasses and garnish each with a slice of lime, lime zest, and a slice of Hatch green chile.

* 6 to 8 fresh limes will produce about 8 oz. of fresh lime juice.

** For less heat and more sweet flavor, reduce the Hatch Simple Syrup to 4 oz. and add 6 oz. of limeade concentrate.

*** For a jalapeño garnish: Delete fresh Hatch green chile and add 1 fresh jalapeño, seeded and sliced.

HATCH APPLETINI

MAKES 1 SERVING

This cocktail is smooth, sweet, and tart all at once. Just a hint of chile creates another layer of sophisticated flavor. Apple and green chile flavor magically complement each other in this cocktail. It is the perfect last-minute martini to enjoy with friends.

> 1 ½ oz. vodka
> 1 oz. apple liqueur
> ½ oz. Hatch Simple Syrup (32)
> Splash of lemon lime soda (optional)
> 1 thin green apple slice

1. Combine vodka, liqueur, and syrup in a cocktail shaker filled with ice.

2. Shake until mixed well, about 1 minute.

3. Pour into a chilled martini glass and top with a splash of lemon lime soda.

4. Garnish with apple slice. Serve immediately.

SPICY MANGO MARGARITA

MAKES 6 SERVINGS

Cool off with a tropical and vibrant margarita. Mangos have a natural richness, which is a bit addictive. Adding a little chile flavor gives this cocktail a fresh and contemporary flavor.

> 3 tbsp. Hatch Red Chile Salt (122)
> 1 tsp. granulated or superfine sugar
> 1 lime, cut into wedges
> 3 cups frozen mango chunks
> 1 cup silver tequila
> 1 cup sugar
> 4 oz. orange-flavored liqueur, such as Triple Sec, Cointreau, or
>   Grand Marnier
> 4 cups cracked ice, divided
> 1 lime sliced into 6 wedges
> 1 fresh mango, peeled and sliced lengthwise

1. Spread red chile salt on a small saucer. Mix in sugar. Rub the rim of each glass with a lime wedge. Dip each glass in salt and sugar mixture and chill in the freezer.

2. In a blender, combine mango, tequila, sugar, and liqueur. Blend until slushy and sugar is dissolved, 2 to 3 minutes. Add ice until desired consistency. Pour into glasses and garnish each with a lime wedge and big chunks of mango.

RASPBERRY CHILE RITA

MAKES 1 SERVING

This is my version of a wonderful berry and chile–infused margarita I have enjoyed for years at La Posta de Mesilla, a historic local restaurant just down the road from Hatch in nearby Las Cruces. The sweetness of this spicy margarita is so inviting. My version combines raspberries and Hatch chile in a special sauce I make with tequila and store-bought margarita mix. If you are a sweet savory lover, this margarita is for you.

> ¼ cup margarita or kosher salt
> 1 lime, cut in 3 wedges, divided
> 1 to 2 oz. silver tequila
> 1 oz. Hatch Chile Raspberry Sauce (119)
> ½ cup prepared margarita mix
> Cracked ice

1. Pour salt across a small saucer or flat surface.

2. Rub rim of glass with lime wedge and dust with salt. Shake off any excess salt.

3. Fill shaker half full of ice. Add tequila and sauce. Add the juice of 2 lime wedges. Top with margarita mix.

4. Shake for 1 to 2 minutes until well blended.

5. Strain over cracked ice in a margarita glass. Garnish with lime wedge.

Variation: For a Frozen Raspberry Chile Rita, place all ingredients in a blender and blend on medium for 2 to 3 minutes until well blended. Pour into salt-rimmed margarita or martini glass and garnish with lime. Double the recipe for 2 margaritas.

(*opposite page*) Frozen Rasperry Chile Rita

WHITE SPICY SANGRIA

I love a refreshing white sangria in the warmer months. This sangria is quick, easy, and so colorful. Adding a spicy kick with my chile-spiked syrup delivers a new elevated flavor. Fresh fruit makes this a beautiful cocktail, so serve it in a large glass pitcher or punch bowl.

⅓ cup brandy
2 bottles (each 750 ml) dry white wine*
8 oz. Hatch Simple Syrup (32)
3 to 4 strawberries, destemmed and thinly sliced
1 cup of blueberries
2 limes, thinly sliced
1 peach, peeled and diced
1 small green apple, cored and thinly sliced
1 bottle (12 oz.) sparkling water

1. In a large pitcher, combine brandy, wine, and syrup.

2. Add fruit and refrigerate overnight.

3. Fill wine glasses or goblets 3/4 full of ice. Pour wine mixture and spoon fruit evenly into each glass. Top each glass with sparkling water

* I like Sauvignon Blanc for this sangria, but experiment with other white wines and find your favorite combination.

MEXICAN MULE

Moscow Mules, typically made with vodka, were invented in the 1940s. They are loved for the ginger beer and the stout copper mugs they are served in. This is my version of an old-style cocktail with a contemporary kick.

½ cup cracked ice
2 oz. tequila
½ oz. fresh lime juice
½ oz. Hatch Simple Syrup (32)
3 oz. ginger beer
Sprig of fresh mint

1. Fill a copper mug half full of ice. Add tequila, lime juice, and syrup and mix well.

2. Top with ginger beer and garnish with fresh mint.

PINEAPPLE CHILE SHANDY

MAKES 1 SERVING

Pineapple and chile make great partners in this cocktail. A shandy is a combination of juice and beer and is such a refreshing sipper. My version takes it up a couple of notches with a bit of vodka and a little heat from the simple syrup.

    2 oz. vodka
    1 oz. Hatch Simple Syrup (32)
    2 oz. pineapple juice
    ¼ oz. fresh lime juice
    Cracked ice
    Light pale ale or beer
    Pineapple wedge

1. In a cocktail shaker add vodka, syrup, pineapple juice, and lime juice. Shake well.

2. Pour into a tall glass ¾ full of ice until it is ¾ full. Top with beer. Garnish with a slice of pineapple.

CHILE-INFUSED VODKA

MAKES 1 QUART

Adding flavor to your favorite liquor is a DIY delight! Infused liquor makes a wonderful gift and is so easy to make. Infusing liquors and simple syrups with chile can really expand your cocktail offerings. Vodka or tequila are a good choice for Hatch chile. Some of my favorites are chile vodka and pineapple, a chile gimlet, and chile vodka with soda and lime. Add this infused liquor to a fun cocktail recipe.

> 1 quart-sized mason jar
> 1 bottle vodka*
> 3 whole fresh, hot Hatch green chiles, destemmed, seeded, and sliced**

1. Place sliced chile in the bottle, cover with vodka, and cover with resealable lid.

2. Place the sealed jar in a cool dark place for 12 to 24 hours.

3. Taste for infused flavor desired. For a stronger flavor, infuse up to 1 week.

4. Strain the infused liquor through a fine mesh sieve into a large glass bowl. To catch any pulp, use a cheesecloth in the sieve.

5. Pour into a quart jar, cover and keep in a cool place or refrigerate for up to a week. Serve in your favorite vodka cocktail.

Variation: For infused tequila: Omit vodka. Replace with tequila and add one whole lime, sliced.

* A high-quality vodka works best.

** Additionally, I like to add a fresh red chile, just before they start to dry in the fall season, for color and a variety of flavor.

HATCH SIMPLE SYRUP

I created this syrup so it can be used to flavor cocktails, iced tea, nonalcoholic drinks, and sauces throughout this cookbook. It is a combination of water, sugar, and Hatch chile. So simple! I encourage you to be creative and find ways to infuse chile into your favorite recipes.

> 1 cup water
> 1 cup sugar
> ½ hot Hatch chile, roasted, peeled, seeded, and chopped

1. In a medium-sized saucepan over medium-high heat, bring water and sugar to a boil until sugar is completely dissolved, about 2 to 3 minutes.

2. Reduce heat and add chile and simmer 5 minutes. Remove from heat and cool.

3. Pour mixture through a fine strainer into a medium-sized bowl. Cool completely. Transfer to a resealable container and refrigerate for up to 2 weeks.

HATCH CHILE FESTIVAL

As New Mexico chile started gaining in popularity, locals felt that Hatch chile needed a bit more recognition for its superior nature. And so a group of local business folks and area farmers created a community event to promote Hatch chile.

"On Labor Day weekend in 1971, the first Annual Chile Festival was held at the Hatch Airport. Farmers, businessmen, various clubs and organizations from the Hatch Valley all worked together organizing booths, entertainment and delicious chile meals serving approximately fifteen hundred people."[1] Since then, this annual festival has grown in size, and Hatch is now known as the "Chile Capital of the World."

Today, this annual Labor Day weekend festival attracts over thirty thousand visitors from around the world. The hometown celebration includes delicious food, queen's court, judged contests, a parade, a carnival, vendors, music and dancing, and LOTS of chile roasting and tasting.

Check your calendar and join the fun!

Note
1. G. Taylor, *History of the Hatch Valley* (Hatch, NM: Hatch Valley Friends of the Library, 1989).

Fun activities for everyone during the Hatch Chile Festival.

2 APPETIZERS AND SHAREABLES

A PICTURESQUE SUNSET EMERGES MOST NIGHTS in the Hatch Valley, as the sun dips behind the mountains and backlights the clouds in red and gold. The warmth of the desert and the coolness of the evenings invite these artistic skies, which crown the farmland and orchards surrounding the village of Hatch.

At the end of a long day working on the farm, Don and Ellie Hackey take time to relax on their front porch overlooking the Hatch Valley. "That view never gets old, we love it," says Don. The Hackeys have been farming in the Hatch Valley for decades, growing lettuce, onions, chile, and pecans.

"We enjoy the soft sounds of nature, seeing the fields full of produce and beautiful orchards moving through the seasons," says Ellie. "This is a perfect place to enjoy a cocktail and a bite to eat at the end of the day."

When planning a get-together with friends or family, you want to start off with great little bites that will get their attention. The following is a collection of Hatch chile–inspired appetizers that are tasty but not difficult. They feature seasonal flavors and the best ingredients, including our own Hatch red and green chile in every form: fresh, dried, or mixed with seasonings and flavorings.

(*opposite page*) Sunset over the Hatch Valley. Courtesy of Ellie Hackey.

BAKED SPICY SWEET POTATO FRIES

MAKES 4 TO 6 SERVINGS

Do you love sweet and savory food combinations? These sweet potato fries tossed in Hatch red chile powder and salt are elevated to sweet-savory heaven—with a little kick, of course. Cotija cheese also adds a salty creamy flavor accent. They are so addicting!

3 to 4 medium sweet potatoes
2 to 3 tbsp. olive oil
2 tsp. Hatch hot red chile powder (Hatch Chile Marketplace, 175)
1 tsp. kosher salt
1 tsp. garlic powder
1 tsp. ground pepper
3 tbsp. cotija cheese
2 to 3 minced green onions

1. Preheat oven to 400 degrees.

2. Peel potatoes and slice each potato into about ¼-inch-thick slices, then cut into fries about ¼ inch in diameter and 3 inches long. Place back in bowl and cover with water.

3. When ready to cook, remove fries from water and pat dry completely with a tea towel or paper towels.

4. Toss fries in a large bowl with oil and spices until well coated.

5. Spread fries evenly across a prepared baking sheet.

6. Bake for 10 minutes until crispy on the bottom. Gently turn over and cook an additional 15 minutes until crispy and brown.

7. Place on a serving dish and garnish with cotija cheese and green onions.

HATCH GREEN AND RED CHILE FRIES

MAKES 4 SERVINGS

Potatoes are our comfort food! They are delicious, easy to prepare, affordable, and so versatile. Pair them with chile and you are in heaven. Chile fries are easy to prepare and delicious.

> 3 to 4 large baking potatoes
> Vegetable oil or peanut oil
> Kosher salt
> Ground black pepper
> 1 cup Hatch green chile, roasted, peeled, seeded, and chopped
> ½ cup Monterey Jack cheese, grated
> ½ cup mozzarella cheese, grated
> ¾ cup Hatch Green Chile Sauce (114) or ¾ cup Hatch Red Chile Sauce (112)
> ¼ cup cotija cheese, crumbled
> 1 tbsp. minced cilantro

1. Peel potatoes and slice each potato into slices about ¼ inch thick, then cut into fries about ¼ inch in diameter and 3 inches long. Place back in bowl and cover with water.

2. When ready to cook, remove fries from water and pat dry completely with a tea towel or paper towels.

3. In a heavy skillet, heat 2 to 3 inches of oil to 300 degrees (use a cooking thermometer to gauge the temperature). Cook small batches of fries until golden brown, about 3 to 5 minutes. Remove and place on a paper towel to drain.

4. (Optional) Increase the heat to 400 degrees and flash fry the fries again until crispy and lightly browned. Remove from oil and place on paper towels.

5. Place freshly cooked fries on a heat-resistant platter and season with salt and pepper to taste.

6. Top with chopped Hatch green chile, spreading evenly. Layer with grated Monterey Jack cheese and grated mozzarella cheese. Place about 6 inches away from the broiler for about 3 to 5 minutes until the cheese is bubbly.

7. Drizzle evenly with ¾ cup warmed Hatch Green Chile Sauce or Hatch Red Chile Sauce.

8. Sprinkle with ¼ cup crumbled cotija cheese and 1 tbsp. minced cilantro.

HATCH PIMENTO SPREAD

MAKES 4 TO 6 SERVINGS

We know that southerners love their pimento cheese. Well, we have our own version and love it just as much! A bit of Hatch chile creates a notable and memorable spread. I love to serve it with fresh crusty sourdough bread, on a sandwich, or just spoon a dollop on a baked potato or cocktail cracker.

> 1 cup mayonnaise
> 1 tsp. Worcestershire sauce
> 1 tsp. minced onion
> One (4-oz.) jar of red pimentos, drained and chopped
> ¼ cup hot Hatch green chile, roasted, peeled, seeded, and minced
> 4 oz. cream cheese (softened)
> 4 cups sharp cheddar cheese, finely grated

1. Using an electric mixer, combine mayonnaise, Worcestershire sauce, onion, pimento, and green chile in a bowl. Mix well with the paddle attachment on medium speed.

2. Slowly add in cheeses and blend on low speed until well blended. Transfer to serving bowl and chill for 1 to 2 hours. Serve with cocktail crackers or as a garnish for potatoes, sandwiches, and more.

Variation: Make Hatch Pimento Sandwiches, a retro 50s classic, for a wedding or baby shower or a light lunch. Take 10 slices of white bread. Spread 5 slices with even amounts of Hatch Pimento Spread. Top with remaining 5 slices of bread. Cut each sandwich diagonally with a serrated knife from corner to corner. Then repeat diagonally in the other direction, corner to corner, creating 4 small triangle sandwiches from each full sandwich. Arrange on a serving platter and enjoy.

PROSCIUTTO AND CHILE BRUSCHETTA

Simple, elegant bites that marry salty with spicy: this little appetizer is great for company but is truly enjoyable at the end of a busy day as an evening snack with a nice glass of wine. Every bite brings together layers of flavor.

> ⅓ cup extra virgin olive oil
> 2 fresh garlic cloves, minced
> 12 slices French baguette bread, sliced ¼ inch thick
> 4 oz. cream cheese
> 12 slices thinly sliced prosciutto
> 2 Hatch green chile, roasted, peeled, seeded, and sliced into ¼-inch strips
> 1 tbsp. chives

1. Preheat oven to 350 degrees.

2. In a small bowl, combine olive oil and garlic. Blend well.

3. Brush each slice of bread with olive oil. Place on a baking sheet and bake until golden brown, about 10 to 12 minutes. Remove from oven and cool completely on a baking rack.

4. Spread each toasted bread slice with a thin layer of cream cheese. Top with a slice of prosciutto and one slice of green chile. Garnish with chives. Place on a serving platter and serve immediately.

HATCH CHILE PECAN CHEESE ROLL

MAKES 4 TO 6 SERVINGS

Chile and pecans are two signature agricultural crops in New Mexico. Whenever I team them together in a recipe it disappears. I use a sharp cheddar and a hot variety of chile for extra flavor. This savory cheese log can be reshaped into a ball, served as a spread, and made ahead of time. Perfect for entertaining year-round.

> 1 cup New Mexico pecans, finely chopped
> One 8-oz. block of cream cheese
> 1 clove garlic, peeled and minced
> Pinch of kosher salt
> 2 cups extra-sharp cheddar cheese, grated
> ½ cup hot Hatch green chile, roasted, peeled, seeded, and minced

1. Preheat oven to 250 degrees.

2. Spread pecans out on a baking sheet and bake for 4 to 5 minutes, just until they become fragrant. Remove from oven and cool. Set aside.

3. In a large mixing bowl, combine cream cheese, garlic, and salt. Mix well.

4. Fold in the cheddar cheese and green chiles. Mix well.

5. Cover and chill in the refrigerator for 2 to 4 hours.

6. Spread toasted pecans on a large cutting board or flat surface.

7. Take cheese mixture out of the refrigerator. With freshly washed and dried hands, form into a log shape about 3 inches by 5 inches.

8. Roll cheese log in toasted pecans, using a spoon to cover the cheese roll if needed, until all sides are covered.

9. Cover the cheese log in foil or plastic wrap and chill for two hours or up to one week in the refrigerator.

10. Serve chilled with cocktail crackers.

Variation: Add 1/4 cup chopped green onion or dried cranberries to cheese mixture when folding in cheddar cheese and green chiles. Follow the rest of the recipe steps.

THE CARSON FAMILY

It all started on the streets of Hatch, New Mexico, in the mid-1950s, prior to a Hatch Valley High School football game. Three years later, Nick Carson, a former football player from El Paso, Texas, married Irene Franzoy, a local farm girl from Hatch, and their journey began.

Over the past sixty-four years, the couple went from farming a fifty-acre farm and selling their vegetables and sun-dried red chile pods in surrounding areas of New Mexico, to running a much more complex, diversified agricultural operation. With the help of their children, grandchildren, and great grandchildren, vegetables, feeds, and red chile spice are still produced on their farms, though they are now distributed across the country and internationally.

Today, Rena and Nick declare that "the love of God, Family, and the Soil" has given them the strength to weather many storms: physical, financial, and natural. When the dust settles and the family gathers for a meal, whether a holiday or regular dinner, there is always a big pan of green chile or a pot of red chile on the table. With lots of onions, of course!

HATCH CHILE ARTICHOKE DIP

MAKES 6 TO 8 SERVINGS

This warm cheesy dip is a classic for family gatherings, happy hours, and game day. My version is spiced up with Hatch chile and fresh garlic. The cream cheese adds depth and creamy texture. So easy! I serve it with corn tortilla chips or bagel chips for a crowd.

1 cup mayonnaise
1 cup and 2 tbsp. finely grated Parmesan cheese, divided
½ cup whipped cream cheese
2 cloves garlic, minced
¼ cup minced white onion
½ cup hot Hatch green chile, roasted, peeled, seeded, and minced
1 cup chopped artichokes hearts, drained and chopped

1. Preheat oven to 350 degrees.

2. Prepare a 9 × 13 in. baking or ovenproof serving dish with cooking spray.

3. In a large mixing bowl, combine mayonnaise, 1 cup of Parmesan, cream cheese, garlic, onion, and green chile. Mix well. Fold in artichokes.

4. Spoon the mixture into the baking dish and sprinkle with remaining Parmesan cheese.

5. Bake for 20 minutes until bubbly in the center and lightly browned around the edges.

6. Serve with warm corn tortilla chips, bagel chips, fresh sourdough bread pieces, or cocktail crackers.

RED CHILE REFRIED BEAN MASH

MAKES 4 TO 6 SERVINGS

Besides the red chile, the best part of this bean dip is the garnish of cilantro, lime, Mexican cheeses, and avocado. Fresh flavors accent the combination of chile and hearty refried beans.

2 cups Refried Beans (264)
⅓ cup Hatch Red Chile Sauce (112)
½ cup sharp cheddar cheese, grated
½ cup Monterey Jack cheese, grated
½ cup cilantro sprigs
1 avocado, seeded, peeled, and sliced
4 to 5 grape tomatoes, sliced
¼ cup cotija cheese, crumbled

1. Spread beans in an 8 × 8 in. heat-resistant baking dish or 6- to 8-inch cast-iron skillet.
2. Spread the red chile sauce over the beans to the edges.
3. Sprinkle the chile bean layers with grated cheeses.
4. Bake for 15 minutes until cheese is melted and bubbly. Remove from oven and let cool for 5 minutes. Garnish with cilantro, avocado, tomatoes and cotija cheese. Serve immediately with corn tortilla chips or cocktail crackers.

CRISPY HATCH CHILE CHEESE BITES

MAKES 4 SERVINGS

This simple low-carb treat is delicious. Crispy rounds of cheese and chile are rich in flavor. I like to add this to my party menu, as there are so many people trying to cut the carbs!

> 1 cup Parmesan cheese, grated
> 1 cup sharp cheddar cheese, grated
> 1 cup Hatch green chile, roasted, peeled, seeded, and cut into ½-inch pieces

1. Preheat oven to 400 degrees.

2. Coat a baking sheet with cooking spray. Place 1 tbsp. of Parmesan cheese on baking sheet and top with 1 tbsp of cheddar cheese, forming a small round. Repeat until you have created 8 piles of cheese, spaced about 3 to 4 inches apart.

3. Place 1 piece of green chile on each round. Watching closely, bake until bubbly and the edges just become browned, about 3 to 4 minutes. Carefully take a knife and push the edges toward the center of each cheese round to keep them from spreading too much. Bake another 3 to 4 minutes.

4. Remove from oven and let cool for 5 to 10 minutes. Cheese rounds should be crispy and firm. Remove from baking sheet with a spatula onto a paper towel to cool. Serve immediately.

HATCH CHILE SPRING ROLLS

MAKES 8 TO 12 SERVINGS

I love it when East meets West in fusion cooking. These filled and rolled appetizers combine fresh vegetables in little bites and are a crowd pleaser. This combination of fresh vegetables and chile neatly wrapped and fried to a crispy finish is delicious.

> 1 cup zucchini, shredded
> 1 cup cabbage, shredded
> 1 carrot, shredded
> ½ cup green chile, roasted, peeled, seeded, and chopped
> Salt and freshly ground black pepper
> 12 spring roll wraps
> Vegetable oil
> Hatch Asian Sauce (101)

1. In a large bowl, combine zucchini, cabbage, and carrot. Add chile and mix well. Season with salt and pepper to taste.

2. To build spring rolls, place 2 heaping tbsp. of vegetable mixture at one end of each spring roll wrap, forming a thin straight line across the end of the spring roll wrap. Fold in both ends and gently roll the wrap and secure with a toothpick.

3. Deep-fry immediately or place spring rolls in a large resealable plastic bag to keep moist and refrigerate until ready to cook or for up to 24 hours.

4. Fill deep skillet or heavy pot with 2 to 3 inches of oil and heat to 300 degrees (use a cooking thermometer to gauge the temperature). Using tongs, gently place 3 to 4 spring rolls at a time in the hot oil and deep-fry, turning once, until crispy and golden brown, 2 to 3 minutes. Drain on paper towels. Season lightly with salt.

HATCH CHILE VERDE CON QUESO

MAKES 4 TO 6 SERVINGS

Queso is loved from coast to coast. Created with so many different cheeses . . . American, asadero, muenster, panela, and Monterey Jack. However, Hatch chile is the star of this appetizer, adding heat and flavor. I have used two basic cheeses in this recipe. I encourage you to experiment and find your favorite. And don't forget to add a garnish or two or three!

> 2 cups cheddar cheese, shredded
> 1 cup Monterey Jack cheese, shredded
> 1 ½ tsp. cornstarch
> ½ cup chicken broth
> 1 ½ cup hot Hatch green chile, roasted, peeled, seeded, and chopped
> 1 tomato, seeded and diced
> ¼ cup milk
> 12-oz. processed cheese product, such as Velveeta, cut into cubes

1. In a large bowl, combine cheddar and Monterey Jack cheeses with cornstarch. Mix well until cheese is well coated.

2. In a large pot, heat broth over medium heat. Sauté chiles and tomato in broth until tomato is soft, 4 to 6 minutes. Reduce heat to medium low and stir in milk and shredded-cheese mixture.

3. Add processed cheese, a few cubes at a time, and stir until smooth. Serve immediately in a heat-resistant bowl. Top with one or more of the garnishes suggested below.

Garnish: ½ cup cooked and crumbled chorizo or spicy sausage, 2 tbsp. Hatch Red Chile Sauce (112) or Hatch Green Chile Sauce (114), 2 to 3 tbsp. sour cream, 2 tbsp. cilantro, a drizzle of Hatch Mexican White Sauce (102), 2 to 3 chopped green onions.

HATCH QUICK QUESO

MAKES 4 TO 6 SERVINGS

There are lots of reasons I developed this "go-to" queso recipe. Queso is always a crowd pleaser, but I don't always have the time to prep a traditional queso. Using store-bought processed Hatch green chile is a time saver and so delicious.

> 1 ½ cups medium or hot processed green chile (Hatch Chile Marketplace, 175)*
> 2 oz. cream cheese
> ¾ cups evaporated milk
> 2 cups medium cheddar cheese, grated
> ¼ tsp. ground black pepper
> ¼ tsp. salt**

1. Heat chile in a skillet over medium heat until heated through.

2. Add cream cheese and evaporated milk, stirring frequently as cream cheese melts.

3. Gradually add grated cheese, salt, and pepper. Stir until it is completely melted.

* For this recipe I like many different prepared sauces, from companies like Ol Gringo, Fresh Chile Company, 505, and Young Guns Chile (just to name a few!), but there are so many delicious options to choose from in the Hatch Chile Marketplace (175).

** I recommend tasting before salting if you are serving with salted corn chips. Less salt can be better.

BAKED QUESO FUNDIDO

This queso is a blend of cheeses and chorizo sausage (a Mexican sausage that is smokey and spicy) baked to bubbly goodness. I make my "bake and serve" queso fundido in an 8-inch skillet, topped with hot green chile and served with fresh garnish. It can be served with corn tortilla chips or folded into fresh, warm corn or flour tortillas.

> 4 oz. chorizo sausage or favorite ground sausage
> 2 cups Monterey Jack cheese, grated
> 2 cups mozzarella cheese, grated
> ½ cup Hatch green chile, roasted, peeled, seeded, and cut into strips or chopped
> ¼ cup minced cilantro
> 1 small tomato, seeded and chopped

1. Preheat oven to 400 degrees.

2. In an 8- or 9-inch cast-iron skillet, cook sausage over medium heat, stirring to keep meat in small crumbles, about 3 to 4 minutes. Remove skillet from heat, then remove and set aside half of the sausage.

3. Spread remaining sausage across the bottom of the skillet.

4. In a medium bowl combine cheeses, mixing well, and spread evenly across the sausage in the skillet. Top evenly with remaining sausage.

5. Gently place green chile across the top of the chorizo.

6. Place skillet in oven and bake for 6 to 8 minutes until cheese is melted, bubbling through the center, and starting to brown on the edges.

7. Garnish with cilantro and tomato and serve immediately.

CHILE CHEESE CRISP

MAKES 4 TO 6 SERVINGS

A lightly toasted flour tortilla topped with melted cheese and a bit of Hatch green chile is so tasty! Toasting the tortilla then adding fresh chile and a pinch of ground black pepper elevates this appetizer. One of life's simple treasures and one of my favorites.

> One 10- to 12-inch flour tortilla
> 1 tsp. butter
> 1 cup (4 oz.) medium cheddar cheese, grated
> 2 tbsp. Hatch green chile, roasted, peeled, seeded, and chopped
> Ground black pepper
> Hatch Green Taco Sauce (86)

1. Preheat broiler, with rack positioned 3 to 4 inches from heat element.

2. Spread one side of tortilla with butter to the edges of the tortilla. Place tortilla, butter side up, on a baking sheet and spread cheese and chile evenly across tortilla to the edges.

3. Broil tortilla until cheese is melted and tortilla is crispy around the edges and slightly brown, 2 to 3 minutes, watching closely.

4. Remove from oven and sprinkle with ground black pepper and drizzle with taco sauce. Slice into 6 wedges.

HATCH RED HONEY CHICKEN QUESADILLA

MAKES 6 WEDGES

There are so many takes on the ever-popular quesadilla, flour tortillas stuffed with cheesy goodness and oozing with flavor. Try my new favorite. Honey, red chile, and chicken gently folded into a flour tortilla filled with melted cheese and grilled to perfection. Unforgettable!

2 tsp. olive oil, divided
1 garlic clove, minced
1 cup chopped cooked chicken
¼ cup Hatch Red Chile Sauce (112)
Two 10-inch flour tortillas
2 cups Monterey Jack cheese, shredded
2 tbsp. honey
2 minced green onion, chopped

1. In a medium skillet sauté olive oil, garlic, and chicken until garlic is softened.

2. Add red chile sauce and cook until heated through. Remove from heat.

3. In a large skillet or griddle, heat 1 tsp. of oil over medium-high heat. Brush to coat pan evenly with oil.

4. Cook one tortilla until air bubbles begin to form, about 1 minute. Turn over and spread half of the cheese evenly over the entire tortilla (do not let tortilla get crispy).

5. Reduce heat to medium and, working quickly, arrange half of the chicken chile mixture over the cheese, then drizzle with 1 tbsp. of honey and half of the green onions. Cook until the cheese starts to melt, about 1 minute, then fold tortilla in half to create a half-moon shape.

6. Turn the folded tortilla over and cook until it is lightly browned and cheese filling is completely melted, 1 to 2 minutes. Transfer quesadilla to a cutting board. Cut into 3 wedges.

7. Add remaining oil to skillet and repeat steps 4 through 6.

HATCH CHILE CHICKEN SLIDERS

MAKES 12 SANDWICHES

Calling all those looking for something hardy to nibble on at a party!
These sliders are just for you. Sliders are easy, versatile, and tasty. Bite-
size party sandwiches wrapped around Hatch chile . . . Yum!

> ½ cup melted butter
> 1 tbsp. brown mustard
> 1 tsp. Worcestershire sauce
> 2 tsp. poppy seeds*
> 2 tbsp. dried onions
> 1 dozen prepared dinner rolls
> ¾ cup mayonnaise
> 2 ½ cups of cooked chicken, shredded**
> 1 cup hot Hatch green chile, roasted, peeled, seeded, and cut into
>   strips or chopped
> ½ lb. thinly sliced provolone cheese

1. Preheat oven to 350 degrees.

2. Place 2 sheets of foil on a baking sheet (2 going lengthwise, 1 going
   crosswise)

3. In a medium-sized mixing bowl, combine butter, mustard, Worcestershire sauce, poppy seeds, and dried onion. Mix well and set aside.

4. Separate the tops of the rolls from bottoms with a serrated knife.

5. Place the bottom buns in the center of the foil on the baking sheet.
   Spread with mayonnaise.

6. Layer the chicken on the bottom half of the rolls. Layer with chile, then
   a layer of sliced cheese. Place tops of the rolls on the sandwiches.

7. Pour mustard mixture evenly over rolls, brushing over each roll. Take
   the foil ends and wrap the sandwiches up to cover and seal all sandwiches and edges.

8. Bake for 18 to 20 minutes. Remove from oven and unwrap foil. Gently
   cut sandwiches with a sharp knife and serve.

Variations: For Hatch Ham Chile Sliders, substitute 1 lb. thinly sliced deli ham for chicken. For Hatch Chile Cheeseburger Sliders, substitute 1 lb. cooked ground beef for chicken and substitute 1/2 lb. thinly sliced American or cheddar cheese for provolone cheese.

* For more flavor omit poppy seeds and add 2 tsp. Everything Bagel seasoning.

** When I am pressed for time, I will use a rotisserie chicken.

HATCH CHILE STUFFED MUSHROOMS

MAKES 6 TO 8 SERVINGS

This meaty appetizer is a family favorite, rich and creamy with a savory spicy flavor. Dried Hatch chile seasonings add that little kick that makes these mushrooms a crowd pleaser.

16 to 20 medium mushroom caps
1 lb. spicy breakfast-style sausage
8 oz. cream cheese, softened
1 tsp. Hatch hot red chile powder (Hatch Chile Marketplace, 175)
½ cup Monterey Jack cheese, shredded
1 tbsp. crushed red pepper flakes
2 tbsp. Parmesan cheese

1. Wash the mushrooms and pat dry with paper towels. Remove the stems and set aside. Preheat oven to 350 degrees.

2. Cook the sausage in a large skillet until done, then drain and place in a mixing bowl. Add the cream cheese, chile powder, Monterey Jack cheese, and crushed red pepper to the bowl. Mix well.

3. Place 1 tsp. of mixture into each mushroom cap. Place the stuffed mushroom caps on a rimmed baking pan, sprinkle all mushrooms with crushed red peppers and Parmesan cheese, and bake for 20 minutes. Remove from oven and let cool for 5 minutes. Serve stuffed mushrooms on a decorative serving platter.

Variation: For a green chile version, omit hot Hatch red chile powder and use ¼ cup Hatch green chile, roasted, peeled, seeded, and minced, instead.

BACON WRAPPED SPICY SHRIMP

MAKES 6 TO 8 SERVINGS

Anything wrapped in bacon is a winner! These little baked shrimp bites have a chile kick and a delicious sweetness. There are so many Hatch chile seasonings to choose from that create intense flavor. They typically are a combination of Hatch chile, salt, pepper, and other spices. Find your favorite in the Hatch Chile Marketplace (175).

> 1 lb. or about 20 large shrimp, peeled and deveined
> 10 slices bacon, cut in half
> 3 tbsp. melted butter
> ¼ cup brown sugar
> 1 tbsp. Hatch chile seasoning

1. Preheat oven to 400 degrees.

2. Wrap each shrimp with ½ slice of bacon and secure with a toothpick. Place on a foil-lined, rimmed baking sheet.

3. In a small bowl combine butter, sugar, and chile seasoning.

4. Use about ½ of the butter mixture to brush each shrimp. Reserve the other half.

5. Bake shrimp until they are pink and opaque, about 10 to 12 minutes. Remove from oven and change the setting to broil.

6. Brush shrimp with remaining butter mixture.

7. Broil for 1 to 2 minutes until browned and bubbly, then turn each shrimp over and broil for another 1 to 2 minutes. Let stand for 5 minutes. Serve warm.

BAKED BRIE AND SWEET CHILE

MAKES 6 TO 8 SERVINGS

I love this simple, yet elegant appetizer. The sweetness of the jam and heat of the chile accent the creamy, rich cheese. I often serve this during the holiday season as a festive appetizer.

> ¼ cup chopped pecans
> One 8-oz. wheel of Brie cheese
> ¼ cup seedless raspberry jam
> ⅓ cup Hatch green chile, roasted, seeded, and chopped
> ½ cup fresh raspberries

1. Preheat oven to 250 degrees. Place pecans on a baking sheet and roast for 4 to 5 minutes until fragrant and toasted. Remove and cool. Increase oven to 375 degrees.

2. Use a sharp knife to remove the top of the rind from the Brie. Place the Brie wheel in an oven-safe dish or small cast-iron skillet, cut side up.

3. Bake at 375 degrees for about 15 minutes until Brie is melted through.

4. While Brie is cooking, combine raspberry jam and green chile over medium-low heat in a small saucepan. Stir until heated through, allowing flavors to blend, about 2 to 3 minutes.

5. Remove Brie from oven and pour raspberry sauce over it. Top with pecans and fresh raspberries. Serve immediately with crackers, sourdough bread pieces, or tortilla chips.

HATCH CHILE CEVICHE

MAKES 4 TO 6 SERVINGS

Ceviche (seh-veey-chay) is a citrus-marinated fish tossed with fresh citrus juices. It is a unique food experience in which the citrus juices cure the fish and cause it to become opaque and firm while absorbing the flavor. Green chile elevates this little dish in so many ways. It is light and refreshing and blends naturally with citrus.

1 lb. halibut steak, cut into bite-size pieces*
Juice of 10 limes
1 medium white onion, finely chopped
4 tomatoes, seeded and finely chopped
1 small yellow chile pepper, seeded and minced
1 cup Hatch green chile, roasted, peeled, seeded, and chopped
1 clove garlic, minced
Kosher salt and freshly ground black pepper
1 tbsp. minced cilantro (optional)
1 bag store-bought corn tortilla chips, warmed

1. In a large bowl, gently combine halibut and lime juice.

2. Add onion, tomatoes, chile, and garlic. Cover and refrigerate, stirring occasionally and allowing flavors to blend, for 2 hours or for up to 4 hours.

3. Just before serving, season with salt and pepper to taste and gently fold in cilantro (optional). Serve with tortilla chips.

Variations: You can use other firm-flesh fish, such as shrimp, scallops, swordfish, cod, catfish, or tilapia.

* Traditionally, ceviche is prepared with raw fish soaking in a citrus bath. However, for food safety purposes, I lightly cook my fish. Bake for 12 minutes at 400 degrees. Allow to cool completely before marinating.

HATCH CHILE WONTONS

MAKES 6 TO 8 SERVINGS

I have been making these wontons for years. A local restauranter gave me the original recipe, and I have spiced it up over time. I like to have a few in the freezer to cook up when guests drop in. These are quick and elegant appetizers that are sure to get your guests' attention.

¼ lb. cheddar cheese, shredded
¼ lb. Monterey Jack cheese, shredded
½ cup Hatch green chile, roasted, peeled, seeded, and minced
½ tsp. salt
¼ tsp. ground black pepper
¼ tsp. cumin
1 glove garlic, chopped
24 wonton wrappers
Flour for dusting
Vegetable oil
Hatch Asian Sauce (101) or Hatch Green Taco Sauce (86)

1. Place cheeses, green chile, salt, pepper, cumin, and garlic in a large mixing bowl and toss gently.

2. Place the wonton wrappers on a clean surface or cutting board, wet the edges with a bit of water, and place a heaping teaspoon of cheese filling in the center of each skin. Fold into a triangle, dampen the edges, and press them together.

3. Dust with flour, repeat the process, and place on a baking sheet and cover until ready to cook.

4. Heat 3 inches of oil over medium-high heat to about 300 degrees (use a cooking thermometer to gauge the temperature). Deep-fry wontons until golden brown (turning from time to time), about 1 to 2 minutes per side. Remove with a slotted spoon onto a paper-toweled surface. Place on a serving platter and serve with salsa or sauces.

HATCH CHILE POTATO SKINS

MAKES 6 SERVINGS

There is something about homemade potato skins . . . they are richer,
crispier, and tastier. A crispy potato skin filled with creamy cheese, chile,
and a fresh garnish is so inviting. Perfect for game night, movie night,
and tailgating.

> 3 medium-sized baking potatoes
> 2 tbsp. olive oil, divided
> 1 cup sour cream
> ¾ cup hot Hatch green chile, roasted, peeled, and seeded
> ⅛ tsp. onion powder
> 1 ½ cup cheddar cheese, grated
> 6 slices of bacon, cooked and crumbled
> 2 green onions, minced

1. Preheat oven to 400 degrees.

2. Rub the skin of the potatoes with 1 tbsp. of olive oil.

3. Place potatoes directly on center rack of oven. Bake for 1 hour until soft
   throughout the center of the potato.

4. While potatoes are cooking, combine sour cream, ¼ cup chile, and
   onion powder in a small bowl and mix well. Cover and chill in the
   refrigerator for 30 minutes or more.

5. Remove potatoes from oven and cool on cutting board.

6. Cut each potato in half, lengthwise. Scoop out most of each center and
   set aside for another recipe, leaving about ¼ of an inch of potato in
   each skin.

7. Brush the inside and rims of each potato half with the remaining olive
   oil. Place on a baking sheet.

8. Top each potato skin with cheese, bacon, green onion, and green chile.

9. Broil for 6 to 8 minutes or until cheese is melted and bacon is crispy and
   heated through. Remove from oven and place on a serving platter. Top
   with sour cream mixture and serve warm.

HATCH CHILE CHICKEN LETTUCE WRAPS

MAKES 4 TO 6 SERVINGS

I love lettuce wraps. They are a low-carb, big-in-flavor delight. Chopped chicken in a rich flavorful sauce with hints of chile makes this appetizer even more delectable. The heat from the chile adds a new dimension to this wrap.

3 tbsp. soy sauce
2 tbsp. packed brown sugar
1 ½ tsp. red wine vinegar
2 tbsp. olive oil, divided
1 lb. boneless skinless chicken breasts, diced into small cubes
1 clove garlic, minced
3 tbsp. minced green onions, white part and a hint of green
1 ¼ cup minced mushrooms
¼ cup hot Hatch green chile, roasted, peeled, and seeded
6 leafy lettuce leaves*

1. For the Stir-Fry Sauce: Combine soy sauce, brown sugar, and vinegar in a small bowl, stirring until sugar dissolves. Set aside.

2. In a large skillet, heat 1 tbsp. of oil over medium-high heat. Add chicken and cook, turning once, until no longer pink inside, 6 to 8 minutes per side.

3. Transfer chicken to cutting board and let cool.

4. In the same skillet, heat remaining tbsp. of oil over medium-high heat.

5. Sauté garlic, green onions, mushrooms, and green chile until onions are tender and transparent and mushrooms are soft, 4 to 5 minutes.

6. Mince chicken and add to the garlic sauté in the skillet. Add Stir-Fry Sauce and sauté chicken mixture over medium heat, until well blended and heated through, 4 to 6 minutes.

7. Place chicken mixture in a serving bowl and lettuce leaves on a serving platter. Allow your guests to serve themselves.

* Boston Bibb or butter lettuce works well for this recipe.

HATCH CHILE NACHOS

MAKES 4 TO 6 SERVINGS

Everyone has a favorite nacho recipe. Originally from Texas, there are now variations of the traditional nacho in eateries around the world—it is a true favorite. Crispy corn tortilla chips and melted cheese always serve as the foundation, and then we get creative. I layer Hatch chile sauce in between chips and cheese and crown it all with fresh Hatch green chile.

> 18 to 24 corn tortilla chips
> 2 cups cheddar cheese, shredded
> 1 cup Monterey Jack cheese, shredded
> ¾ to 1 lb. cooked chicken, steak, or ground beef,* warmed
> ½ cup hot Hatch green chile, roasted, peeled, seeded, and chopped
> ¼ cup Hatch Green Taco Sauce (86)
> ½ cup Hatch Chile Guacamole (84) or store-bought guacamole
> ⅓ cup pickled jalapeño pepper slices, drained
> ⅓ cup sliced black olives, drained
> 1 tomato, seeded and diced
> ¼ cup Hatch Mexican White Sauce (102)

1. Preheat oven to 350 degrees.

2. Place tortilla chips on an ovenproof platter. Top chips evenly with half of the cheese.

3. Top with chicken or beef, remaining cheese, and chile. Bake until cheese is melted and bubbling throughout, 6 to 8 minutes, and remove from oven.

4. Top with a drizzle of taco sauce, guacamole, jalapeños, olives, and tomato, then drizzle with white sauce.

Variations: For Red Chile Nachos: Omit Hatch green chile and Hatch Green Taco Sauce and add 1/2 cup Hatch Red Chile Sauce (112) or a store-bought chile sauce, heated. Once nachos are melted and bubbling, remove them from oven and drizzle with sauce. Continue with step 3.
* Toppings: Try a variety of proteins: 1 lb. of shredded rotisserie chicken, cooked thinly sliced grilled steak, or 1 lb. cooked ground beef seasoned to taste.

HATCH CHILE PINWHEELS

MAKES 4 TO 6 SERVINGS

Little bites of soft cheese filling spiked with Hatch green chile rolled in a soft flour tortilla are the ultimate appetizer. Simple, tasty, and addictive! These classic green chile spirals taste best with hot Hatch green chile accenting the creamy filling of this make-ahead tidbit.

½ cup Hatch green chile, roasted, peeled, seeded, and minced
1 tsp. granulated garlic
Pinch of salt
8 oz. cream cheese
Four 10-inch flour tortillas
Crushed red pepper (optional)
Cilantro, minced (optional)

1. Combine green chile, garlic, and salt in a medium bowl with the cream cheese. Mix well.

2. Using 2 to 3 tbsp. per tortilla, spread the mixture out to the outer edges of each tortilla.

3. Roll up tightly, making sure each tortilla ends up as an even, round tube shape. Place the rolled tortillas in a large resealable bag or plastic wrap and refrigerate for 3 hours or up to 2 to 3 days.

4. Before serving, slice into ¼-inch rounds and arrange on a platter. Sprinkle with crushed red pepper and/or fresh cilantro.

SAVORY CHILE CHEESECAKE

MAKES 6 TO 8 SERVINGS

This savory chile cheesecake is easy and elegant. This showstopper is
a holiday or special occasion classic, featuring rich and creamy cheese
filling layered and spiked with spicy chile and sweet red peppers. Serve to
satisfy and impress.

> ½ lb. provolone, thinly sliced
> 8 oz. cream cheese, softened
> 2 tbsp. butter
> ½ cup prepared basil pesto
> ¼ cup pecans, toasted and chopped
> 1 red bell pepper, roasted
> 4 oz. hot Hatch green chile, roasted, peeled, seeded, and chopped

1. Line a 7-inch springform pan with plastic wrap, leaving plenty of over-
   hang on each side. Place the cheese slices on the bottom and up the
   sides of the pan, overlapping for complete coverage.

2. In a stand mixer, combine the cream cheese and the butter on medium-
   low speed with a paddle attachment. Add the pesto and mix well.

3. Spread ⅓ of the creamy pesto mixture on the provolone, then sprinkle
   with ⅓ of the pecans, ⅓ of the red pepper, and ⅓ of the green chile.
   Repeat twice and finish with a layer of provolone.

4. Cover completely with plastic wrap, sealing all edges. Gently press
   down and refrigerate for 8 to 12 hours.

5. Remove from refrigerator and remove the plastic wrap from the top. In-
   vert the cheese round onto a serving platter. Remove the plastic wrap
   and slice half the round into thin wedges. Arrange these slices around
   remaining uncut cheese round. Serve at room temperature, slicing
   more as needed.

THE HACKEY FAMILY

At the end of his senior year, as WWII raged across the globe, Ralph Hackey joined the US Air Force and flew numerous missions over Europe. After being discharged, he came back to New Mexico, married his college sweetheart, Mary Ruth Simpson, and bought a farm in Rincon, near Hatch. With their young family, Linda, Jim, and Don, they farmed cotton, alfalfa, lettuce, cayenne, jalapeno cherry peppers, banana peppers, watermelon, and pumpkins through the years. In the mid-1980s, they started growing Hatch chile, then they invested in a dehydrating company, a chile spice company, and many other chile endeavors. More recently, the Hackeys have moved into growing pecans. Today, Don Hackey and his wife Ellie and their growing family continue to farm in the valley. They enjoy Hatch and call it home.

HATCH CHILE FETA CROSTINI

MAKES 4 TO 6 SERVINGS

Such a colorful appetizer! Layers of flavor are piled on lightly toasted rounds in a dish that is easy to make and fun to serve. Fresh roasted Hatch chile and a garnish of basil add the crowning touch.

> 6 oz. crumbled feta cheese
> 2 oz. cream cheese
> Juice of 1 lemon
> ½ cup olive oil
> Pinch of kosher salt
> Pinch of fresh ground pepper
> 20 slices French baguette bread, sliced into ¼-inch slices, lightly toasted
> 1 cup green chile, roasted, peeled, seeded, and minced
> 10 to 15 grape tomatoes, cut in half diagonally
> 2 tbsp. minced fresh basil

1. Place feta and cream cheese in a food processor and pulse until well blended.

2. Slowly add lemon juice, olive oil, salt, and pepper (to taste), and pulse until blended smooth.

3. Spread feta cheese mixture on toasted bread. Place on a serving platter. Top evenly with green chile and tomato on bread slices. Garnish with basil and serve.

HATCH RED CHILE MEATBALL BITES

MAKES 4 TO 6 SERVINGS

Creating a unique red sauce makes these meatballs a party favorite. Homemade meatballs drenched in a sweet spicy sauce! I love adding three types of garnish for visual appeal and to enhance the flavor.

  1 lb. lean ground beef
  1 large egg, beaten
  ¼ cup bread crumbs
  ¼ cup plus 2 tbsp. grated Parmesan cheese, divided
  2 cloves garlic, minced
  ¾ tsp. kosher salt
  1 cup Hatch Red Chile Sauce (112)
  1 cup prepared spaghetti or marinara sauce
  2 green onions, minced
  1 tbsp. Italian flat parsley, minced

1. Preheat oven to 400 degrees. Line a rimmed baking sheet with foil.

2. In a large bowl, combine ground beef, egg, bread crumbs, ¼ cup Parmesan cheese, garlic, and salt. Mix well. Add 1 tbsp. of water if you need it moistened.

3. Form meatballs into 1½-inch balls and place on baking sheet.

4. Bake for 10 minutes. Turn each meatball once and bake another 7 minutes until barely pink inside.

5. Place red chile sauce and spaghetti sauce in a large skillet and simmer over medium-low heat. Gently add meatballs to the sauce. Simmer on low until the meatballs are heated through. Transfer to a serving bowl and garnish with remaining Parmesan cheese, onion, and parsley.

HATCH CHILE CHEESE PUFF

MAKES 4 TO 6 SERVINGS

If you are a pastry lover and a chile lover you will be in heaven. These flaky, rich, and cheesy pastries are addicting! Puff pastry sheets make this elegant appetizer easy to make.

1 egg, beaten
2 tbsp. water
1 package puff pastry sheets (2 in a package), thawed
1 ½ cups green chile, roasted, peeled, seeded, and chopped
2 cups sharp cheddar cheese, grated
Kosher salt

1. Preheat oven to 400 degrees. Line a rimmed baking sheet with parchment paper.

2. Beat the egg and water in a small bowl until well blended.

3. Unfold 1 pastry sheet on a cutting board and cut in half. Then arrange both halves of the pastry sheet on the baking sheet.

4. Arrange the green chile and cheese on top of each pastry sheet to within 1 inch of the edge.

5. Sprinkle lightly with salt.

6. Brush the edges with the egg mixture.

7. Unfold the second pastry sheet on a cutting board and cut in half. Place each sheet on top of the chile and cheese. Crimp the edges with a fork, sealing the edges of each pastry.

8. Brush the edges and the tops of both pastries with the remaining egg mixture. Using a sharp knife, cut 6 to 8 slits in the top of the pastry. Sprinkle with kosher salt.

9. Bake for 22 to 28 minutes until light and golden brown. Remove from oven and let cool for 15 to 20 minutes. Slice in squares and serve.

MINI CHILE CORN FRITTERS

MAKES 4 SERVINGS

These little fritters are crispy and spicy. Chile and corn go together in a blended harmony of flavor. Add a little batter and fry them up for pure comfort food.

> 1 ½ cups frozen sweet corn kernels, thawed
> 2 tbsp. minced green onion, divided
> ¼ cup green chile, roasted, peeled, seeded, and minced
> 1 cup pancake batter, mixed as directed
> ½ tsp. salt
> ¼ tsp. ground black pepper
> 1 tbsp. butter
> ½ cup sour cream
> 1 tbsp. minced cilantro
> 1 tbsp. minced Italian parsley

1. In a medium bowl combine corn, onion, and green chile. Gently fold in the pancake batter, salt, and pepper.

2. Heat a large skillet over medium heat and brush with melted butter. Place a heaping tbsp. of batter in the skillet. Cook until pancake bubbles up, about 2 to 3 minutes, then flip and cook until golden brown on each side. Remove from skillet.

3. Place on a serving platter. Serve warm, with a dab of sour cream on each fritter. Garnish evenly with cilantro and parsley.

DIY CHILE CHIPS

MAKES 36 CHIPS, 6 TO 8 SERVINGS

We start most meals with a bowl of fresh chips and a side of salsa in our region. It's easy to buy a bag of chips, but the best corn tortilla chips are homemade. These crispy fried chips are so delicious and elevate the flavor of any salsa, queso, or nacho.

> Oil
> Eight 6-inch corn tortillas, each cut into 6 wedges
> Salt
> Hatch red or green chile seasoning (Hatch Chile Marketplace, 175)

1. Fill a deep-fryer, deep heavy pot, or deep skillet with 3 inches of oil and heat to 350 degrees. Using tongs, gently place 4 to 6 tortilla wedges at a time in the hot oil and deep-fry, turning once, until crisp, about 1 to 2 minutes. Drain on paper towels.

2. Season with salt and chile seasonings.

3 SALSAS, SAUCES, AND CULINARY ACCENTS

PEOPLE ARE CRAZY ABOUT CONDIMENTS; we do crazy things with them. We put ketchup on scrambled eggs, salsa in soups, ranch dressing on pizza. It's a culinary game, and we just keep experimenting more and more. We are no less obsessed with adding Hatch chile to this game. Creating condiments with red and green Hatch chile expands the condiment horizon in many ways. First, there is the chile flavor: green, crisp, and fresh or red, rich, and earthy. Second, chile enhances texture by adding chopped, minced, or pureed consistencies to any recipe. Third, varying the heat level from mild to medium to hot alters not only spiciness but flavor. Finally, with processed chile, there are so many opportunities to experiment with the powders, chile flakes, and seasoning mixes.

I created this collection salsas, sauces, relishes, and moles to accent delicious entrées, sides, appetizers, and more. By simply pairing some of these with good, sound recipes you can bring out their full flavor. So, dive into your favorites but also explore new ones and drizzle, spread, plop, scoop, smear, dollop, and pour a bit more flavor on top.

(*opposite page*) Fresh red and green chile ristras, drying in the sun at a roadside stand in Hatch, New Mexico.

HATCH TABLE SALSA

MAKES 2 CUPS

This basic table salsa is an everyday condiment in our house. For the best flavor and brightest color, I use canned tomatoes teamed with fresh Hatch green chile. This creates a consistency of tomato flavor in this salsa. At times, I do like to add a little extra spice and texture with crushed chile peppers. My girlfriends and I have been making this salsa for years, serving it with EVERYTHING, and dipping in with corn tortilla chips or even saltines on a summer afternoon. Crown a sizzlin' burger or seared steaks with this mouthwatering goodness.

> 1 can (28 oz.) diced tomatoes, muddled*
> 1 ½ cups Hatch green chile, roasted, peeled, seeded, and chopped
> 3 to 4 green onions, minced
> 1 medium onion, finely chopped
> 1 clove garlic, minced
> ½ tsp. crushed red pepper flakes (optional)
> Kosher salt
> Splash of wine vinegar or fresh lime juice (optional)

1. In a large bowl, combine tomatoes, chiles, both types of onions, garlic, red pepper flakes, and salt to taste. Add splash of vinegar or lime juice. Mix well.

2. Transfer to an airtight container and refrigerate, stirring occasionally, for 30 minutes or for up to 2 days.

Variation: For a completely different and finer texture, combine all of the ingredients except the lime juice/vinegar. Pour into food processor and pulse for 1 to 2 minutes until smooth. Add a splash of lime juice or vinegar. For a thinner salsa, add 1/2 cup water when combining ingredients.
* I like to muddle the tomatoes a bit for a thicker texture.

(*opposite page, clockwise*) Chile Avocado Salsa, Hatch Chile Come Back Sauce, Chile Mustard, Hatch Asian Sauce, Spicy Veggie Salsa, and Hatch Green Taco Sauce (center).

HATCH HARVEST SALSA

MAKES 2 CUPS

Roasted tomato adds a depth of flavor to this garden-fresh salsa. The slightly charred flakes from the skin of the charred tomatoes disperses among the chiles, onions, and tomato base, adding a new level of dippable flavor.

> 6 fresh homegrown or vine ripe tomatoes, cored and sliced in half
> 1 yellow onion, sliced into 4 to 6 slices
> 4 garlic cloves, chopped
> 3 green onions, green parts only, finely chopped
> 1 tsp. minced cilantro (optional)
> ½ cup Hatch green chile, roasted, peeled, seeded, and finely chopped
> Pinch of kosher salt

1. Place tomatoes, skin side up, onion slices, and garlic cloves on a baking sheet and broil until skins are charred and blistered, about 6 to 8 minutes. Remove from oven and cool.

2. In a blender or food processor, pulse charred tomatoes, onion, and garlic until blended but chunky, about 2 to 3 minutes.

3. Pour into a medium-sized bowl and fold in green onions, cilantro, green chile, and salt to taste. Mixture will be thick and slightly chunky.

4. Serve immediately or transfer to an airtight container for up to 2 days.

Variations: For additional flavor, add 1 tbsp. minced fresh cilantro when mixing ingredients in the blender or food processor. For a finer, taco-style sauce, add green onions, cilantro, and green chile to the blender or food processor and pulse until smooth, about 4 to 6 minutes.

RICH CORN RELISH

MAKES 2 CUPS

This corn salsa delivers layers of flavor with a creamy, tangy sauce flecked with fresh red onion and chile. It is a sweet blend I like to fold into a roasted pork soft taco or spread across a warm flour tortilla for an afternoon snack.

> ¼ cup mayonnaise
> 2 tbsp. sour cream
> ½ tsp. ground cumin
> 1 tbsp. fresh lime juice
> 1 ½ cups corn kernels*
> ¼ cup minced red onion
> ½ cup Hatch green chile, roasted, peeled, seeded, and chopped
> Freshly ground black pepper
> Pinch of kosher salt

1. In a large bowl, combine mayonnaise, sour cream, cumin, and lime juice. Add corn, onion, and chile. Toss gently until well coated.

2. Season with black pepper and salt to taste. Serve immediately or transfer to an airtight container and refrigerate for up to 2 days.

* You can use frozen corn, thawed; canned corn, drained; or cooked corn from the cob.

HATCH CHILE SALSA VERDE

MAKES 2 CUPS

The naturally tart flavors of tomatillos, green chile, and cilantro are a favorite in this region. A splash of fresh lime juice enhances the tomatillo flavor to create a light citrus salsa. I roast half the tomatillos for a charred flavor, keeping the other half fresh for texture.

8 to 10 tomatillos, dried skins removed, divided
2 tbsp. olive oil
2 cloves garlic, minced
½ cup green chile, roasted, peeled, seeded, and chopped
1 small white onion, chopped
Juice of 2 limes
¼ cup fresh cilantro, chopped (optional)
Kosher salt

1. In a skillet over high heat, sear half the tomatillos until soft, charred, and bubbling. Remove from heat and cool.

2. In a blender or food processor, pulse together all tomatillos, oil, garlic, chile, onion, lime juice, and cilantro until slightly chunky. Pour into a serving bowl. Add salt to taste.

3. Refrigerate for 1 hour or transfer to an airtight container and refrigerate for up to 24 hours.

CHILE AVOCADO SALSA

MAKES 1 ½ CUPS

This colorful classic stands alone as a dip with chips or as a culinary accent for so many favorites. I love this avocado chile combination spooned across my tacos, nachos, grilled and roasted meats, and pasta. Fresh avocado brings it all together for a creamy smooth finish.

3 to 4 tomatillos
½ medium onion, chopped
¼ cup cilantro, minced
½ cup Hatch green chile, roasted, peeled, seeded, and chopped
2 garlic cloves
1 medium avocado, pitted, peeled, and diced
½ tsp. kosher salt

1. In a skillet over high heat, sear tomatillos and onion until soft, charred, and bubbling. Remove from heat and cool.

2. In a blender or food processor, combine tomatillos, onion, cilantro, chile, and garlic and pulse for 1 minute, until blended.

3. Add avocado and salt and pulse until smooth, about 2 minutes. Serve immediately or transfer to an airtight container and refrigerate for up to 2 days.

HATCH CHILE GUACAMOLE

MAKES 4 TO 6 SERVINGS

Guacamole is versatile and can be used as a garnish or an appetizer. This classic version works for both. Smooth avocado and chile pair well together. Serve it with warm corn tortilla chips or garnish your favorite burrito or taco recipe.

6 avocados, mashed
1 cup Hatch green chile, roasted, peeled, seeded, and chopped
1 tomato, seeded and chopped
¼ cup minced onion
2 tbsp. freshly squeezed lime juice
½ tsp. salt
¼ tsp. black pepper

1. In a large bowl, gently combine avocados, chile, tomato, and onion. Add lime juice and mix well. Season with salt and pepper and serve immediately or transfer to an airtight container and refrigerate for 30 minutes or for up to 2 hours.

SPICY VEGGIE SALSA

MAKES 2 CUPS

This medley of veggies adds a zesty freshness to most any entrée, grilled fish, chicken, and even pasta. I will heap a bit on a warm corn tortilla chip as an afternoon appetizer. . . . so good!

    3 green onions, minced
    2 yellow squash, chopped into ¼-inch pieces
    2 medium zucchinis, chopped into ¼-inch pieces
    1 medium red bell pepper, chopped
    2 tbsp. olive oil
    1 tsp. kosher salt
    1 to 2 tsp. Hatch red chile powder (Hatch Chile Marketplace, 175)

1. In a medium bowl, gently combine onions, squash, zucchini, bell pepper, and olive oil. Toss until well coated.
2. Sprinkle with salt and chile powder and gently mix well. Serve immediately or transfer to an airtight container and refrigerate for up to 2 days.

HATCH GREEN TACO SAUCE

MAKES 2 CUPS

From taco trucks to a little diner down the road all along the border, we often go back for the taco sauce or salsa. Typically, it is a red tomato–based sauce, but try my green chile version, which adds a different dimension of flavor, equally relevant in the taco-sauce space.

1 cup Hatch green chile, roasted, peeled, seeded, and minced
2 cloves garlic, minced
2 tbsp. olive oil
1 cup water
½ medium white or yellow onion, minced
Juice of 1 small lime
1 tsp. kosher salt

1. In a blender or food processor, pulse green chile, garlic, olive oil, and water.

2. Add onion, lime juice, and salt. Pulse until smooth, about 2 minutes.

3. Transfer to an airtight container or bottle.

4. Refrigerate for 2 hours or for up to 2 days.

Tip: For a richer chile flavor, add 1 additional cup of green chile and ½ cup of water in step 1.

HATCH GREEN CHILE RELISH

MAKES 2 CUPS

This relish is simple, tasty, and versatile. It is another Hatch-inspired condiment laced with garlic and oregano. I have made this relish with green chile, fresh-roasted red chile, and the autumn-blend roast, which is picked right when the green chile starts turning to red. I love it on a char-cuterie board with crackers and cheese or piled high on a steak or grilled chicken breast.

> 2 cups Hatch green chile, roasted, peeled, seeded, and chopped*
> ¼ cup olive oil
> 5 cloves garlic, minced
> 1 tsp. crushed Mexican oregano**
> Kosher salt

1. In a large bowl, combine chiles, oil, garlic, oregano, and salt to taste.

2. Let stand at room temperature for 30 minutes, stirring occasionally. Serve immediately or transfer to an airtight container and refrigerate, stirring occasionally, for 1 hour or for up to 2 days.

* Substitute Bueno® autumn-roast chile for green chile or use 1 cup fresh green chile and 1 cup fresh red chile.

** Mexican oregano is a bit more pungent than regular oregano. You can find Mexican oregano at your local market in the Mexican food section.

REALLY RED ONION RELISH

MAKES 2 ½ CUPS

Growing up in the agricultural industry, we had potatoes and onions at almost every meal. My mother fixed them in every way imaginable. My dad loved onions raw, grilled, baked, broiled, or marinated. This is my version of his favorite condiment—marinated onions with a dash of red chile.

> 2 large red onions, cut in half and thinly sliced
> 1 cup red wine vinegar
> 2 tbsp. water
> 2 tbsp. sugar
> 1 tbsp. Hatch red chile powder (Hatch Chile Marketplace, 175)

1. In a large bowl, combine onion slices, vinegar, and water.

2. In a small bowl combine sugar and red chile powder. Mix well and sprinkle over onions.

3. Toss onions and chile mixture until sugar is dissolved.

4. Chill for 2 hours, stirring occasionally. Transfer to an airtight container and refrigerate for 1 hour or for up to 24 hours.

THE SHIFLETT FAMILY

In 1968 Francis and Nelda Shiflett moved their family from Texas to the Uvas Valley, southwest of Hatch. They were dryland farmers looking for water, and they found it, as well as the opportunity to grow new crops. This was the beginning of Shiflett Produce.

Today, brothers Dale and Gary Shiflett continue to farm this valley. Through the years, they have put in irrigation systems, upgraded their packing facilities, and expanded the crops they grow, which now include a variety of feed crops along with onions and chile. Tyrell, Clayton, and Cody farm alongside their father, Dale. In 2018 Dale and the boys opened a fresh chile packing shed in the valley.

The valley has been their home for over fifty years. "It's a true agriculture community whose roots run deep with core values and a shared passion for being stewards of the land," notes Cody Shiflett.

Cody's wife, Dru, shared that their go-to chile favorite is a simple fresh green and red chile, roasted, peeled and chopped, mixed with fresh-minced garlic: "We top anything and everything, or just eat it with chips or a tortilla. We prep this chile mix in large quantities during chile season and have a freezer full at all times."

Shiflett Produce crew harvesting Hatch chile. Photo courtesy of Dru Shiflett.

89

SIMPLY PICKLED ONIONS

Pickled onions can elevate an entire entrée. Here is my favorite version.

    1 red onion
    Juice of 2 medium lemons

1. Slice onion into thin slices, creating rings. Place in an airtight container and squeeze lemon juice over the top. Cover and shake. Refrigerate overnight, shaking occasionally. Garnish your favorite dish with this fresh citrusy flavor!

CHILE-SPICED CARAMELIZED ONIONS

Caramelized onions are rich in flavor and add so much to entrées, burgers, sandwiches, burritos, and more. Sweet, savory, and spicy, Hatch chile style is what you will get with this recipe.

> 2 tbsp. olive oil
> 2 large onions, thinly sliced in rings
> 1 tbsp. Worcestershire sauce
> 1 tbsp. sugar
> ½ tsp. Hatch red or green chile powder (Hatch Chile Marketplace, 175)
> 1 tsp. crushed red chile flakes
> Splash of liquid*

1. In a large skillet, heat oil over medium-high heat and add onions. Cook for 2 to 3 minutes until they start to soften.

2. Add Worcestershire sauce, sugar, and spices. Stir until onions are well coated and slowly becoming transparent. Scrape the bottom and sides of skillet as the onions caramelize.

3. Add a splash of liquid to sauté and stir until onions are transparent, dark, and a bit charred, about 14 to 16 minutes.

4. Remove from heat and serve immediately.

* Add just a splash of your choice: balsamic vinegar, bourbon, red wine, or light beer.

PICKLED HATCH GREEN CHILE

MAKES 1 PINT JAR

How about a spicy pickled pepper? Yes, fresh Hatch chiles cured in a light vinegary solution create the best pickled peppers. Perfect with a sandwich or on a burger, or you can add a few to your next charcuterie board or top your next salad with flavor.

    1 cup white vinegar
    1 cup water
    1 tbsp. salt
    2 tbsp. sugar
    3 cloves garlic, minced
    ¼ tsp. red pepper flakes
    3 whole Hatch chiles, destemmed, seeded, and sliced
        into ¼-inch rings
    1 medium onion, sliced

1. In a small saucepan, combine vinegar, water, and salt. Add sugar, garlic, and pepper flakes and bring to a boil.

2. Add chile and onion. Boil for 2 minutes, remove from heat, and cool for 5 to 8 minutes.

3. Gently, place chiles and onions in a mason jar.

4. Pour brine over chiles to fill the jar.

5. Cool to room temperature. Refrigerate for up to 2 weeks.

HATCH CHILE AND JALAPEÑO JELLY

MAKES 5 HALF-PINT JARS

Food gifting is a love of mine. This shelf-stable jelly can be enjoyed year-round and makes a wonderful gift from the kitchen. The combination of jalapeños and Hatch chile elevates the heat just enough. Sweet savory jelly is delicious over cream cheese for a simple appetizer or as a glaze over salmon or grilled chicken.

Five (8-oz.) half-pint glass preserving jars with lids and bands
6 medium-heat jalapeños, stemmed and seeded
½ cup hatch green chile, roasted, peeled, seeded, and minced
2 cups cider vinegar, divided
6 cups sugar
Two (3-oz.) pouches of liquid pectin
½ tbsp. Kosher salt
Green food coloring (optional)

1. Prepare a large pot with 2 to 3 inches of boiling water. Heat jars in simmering water until ready for use.

2. Puree jalapeños and green chile in a food processor or blender with 1 cup of cider vinegar until smooth. Do not strain.

3. Combine puree with remaining vinegar and sugar in a saucepan. Bring to a boil over high heat. Boil for 10 minutes while stirring.

4. Add both packets of pectin and salt and boil for 1 more minute, stirring constantly. Remove from heat. Add food coloring (if using) and stir. Skim foam off the top if needed.

5. Take each jar out of simmering water and dry off with a paper towel. Ladle hot mixture into warm jars leaving ¼-inch headspace. Wipe rim, place lid on jar, and apply the band until fit is tight.

6. Place jars back in pot with boiling water, making sure water covers most of each jar. Set in boiling water for 10 minutes. Remove jars and cool. Check lids for seal after 24 hours.

ORANGE CHILE GLAZE

MAKES 1 ½ CUPS

Orange is a wonderful flavor blend for spicy green chile. This easy sweet-savory glaze is delicious on baked ham or grilled pork chops, or you can just pour it over cream cheese as an appetizer.

> 1 tbsp. olive oil
> 4 garlic cloves, minced
> 1 cup prepared orange marmalade
> 1 cup Hatch green chile, roasted, peeled, seeded, and minced
> 4 oz. white wine

1. In a small saucepan sauté oil and garlic over medium-low heat until soft, about 1 minute.

2. Add marmalade, chile, and wine, stirring constantly until well blended, about 5 to 7 minutes. Serve immediately or cool to room temperature and transfer to an airtight container and refrigerate for 2 to 3 days.

HATCH HOT HONEY

MAKES ½ CUP

Sweet, spicy honey is thoughtful and intriguing. Drizzle and drip across pizza, crostini, or roasted or grilled chicken. I often serve it with a basket of rustic breads or fresh-baked biscuits. Local honey is a great choice, as it usually contains local pollen, which can help during allergy season.

> 2 tsp. hot sauce*
> 1 tsp. Hatch hot red chile powder (Hatch Chile Marketplace, 175)
> ½ cup honey

1. In a small bowl, combine chile powder and chile sauce. It will become thicker, creating a paste. Stir until well blended.

2. Pour honey into a small saucepan over low heat. Slowly add chile paste, stirring to blend. Cool and use immediately or transfer to an airtight container and refrigerate for up to 1 month.

Variation: For a different red chile flavor, decrease hot sauce to 1 tsp., omit Hatch red chile powder, and add 1 tbsp. of Hatch Red Chile Sauce (112, or Hatch Chile Marketplace, 175).

* I like Louisiana Hot Sauce or Cholula Sauce. Increase honey by ¼ cup for a sweeter experience.

HATCH BACON JAM

MAKES 1 CUP

This slow-simmering, sweet, and savory jam accents almost anything. The caramelized onions and bacon are rich in flavor. Serve it over Brie or spoon it across grilled meats or poultry. Surprise your guests by upscaling a sandwich or burger with this savory jam.

8 slices bacon, cut into ¼-inch pieces
1 large onion, thinly sliced
½ cup brown sugar
1 tsp. Hatch red or green chile powder (Hatch Chile Marketplace , 175)
2 tbsp. apple vinegar
¼ tsp. granulated garlic
2 tbsp. honey

1. In a medium skillet, cook bacon pieces over medium-high heat. Cook for 8 to 10 minutes until done. Some pieces will be crispy, and some will still be soft but firmly cooked. Remove bacon pieces from the skillet with a slotted spoon to a paper towel.

2. Drain all but 2 tbsp. of bacon fat from skillet and reduce heat to medium low. Add onion slices and cook, stirring constantly, until onions have caramelized, about 18 to 20 minutes.

3. Add the reserved bacon pieces, sugar, chile powder, vinegar, granulated garlic, and honey and increase heat to medium. Cook for 25 to 30 minutes until mixture is thick. Serve immediately or cool to room temperature and transfer to an airtight container and refrigerate for up to 3 days.

Variation: For a thicker, spicy jam omit the chile powder and add ¼ to ½ cup Hatch green chile, roasted, peeled, seeded, and minced. Follow recipe as directed.

HATCH VINAIGRETTE

MAKES 1 CUP

Spice up your greens with a little Hatch chile! This vinaigrette, green or red, is so versatile. Besides a drizzle on my salads, veggies, and sandwiches, I use it to marinate steak, dress a bowl of pasta, flavor grilled chicken, and as a dipper for my fresh veggies.

> 2 tbsp. minced onion
> ⅓ cup cider vinegar
> 1 clove garlic, minced
> 2 tbsp. honey
> 1 tsp. salt
> 1 tbsp. brown mustard
> ¾ cup olive oil
> ⅓ cup Hatch green chile, roasted, peeled, seeded, and minced

1. In a food processor, combine onion, vinegar, garlic, honey, and salt.
2. Slowly pulse on low while adding mustard, olive oil, and chile. Blend until smooth. Serve immediately or transfer to an airtight container and refrigerate for 2 to 3 days.

Variation: For Red Chile Vinaigrette: Omit mustard and green chile and add 1 ½ tsp. Hatch red chile powder (Hatch Chile Marketplace, 175).

HATCH RED CHILE BBQ SAUCE

MAKES 3 CUPS

Much like salsa, barbeque sauce is so personal. What I do know is that it adds a special flavor to every plate of grilled meats and chicken. This is my southern specialty, Hatch style, rich and spicy.

1 tbsp. olive oil
1 small onion, chopped
1 jalapeño pepper, stemmed, seeded, and minced
2 cloves garlic
2 ½ cups ketchup
½ cup Hatch Red Chile Puree (117, or Hatch Chile Marketplace, 175)
¾ cup firmly packed brown sugar
1 cup apple cider vinegar
⅓ cup honey
1 tbsp. Worcestershire sauce
1 tsp. kosher salt
½ tsp. ground black pepper
1 tsp. Hatch red chile powder (Hatch Chile Marketplace, 175)

1. Heat oil over medium-low heat in a saucepan and sauté onion, jalapeño, and garlic until softened, about 2 to 3 minutes.

2. Stir in ketchup, chile puree, brown sugar, vinegar, honey, Worcestershire sauce, salt, pepper, and chile powder.

3. Bring sauce to a boil for 2 minutes. Reduce heat and simmer on low for 30 minutes, stirring occasionally. Serve immediately or cool to room temperature and transfer to an airtight container and refrigerate for up to 1 week.

HATCH CHILE DIPPING OIL

MAKES 1 CUP

This dipping oil has such a rich combination of herbs, fresh garlic, and chile. Drizzle a little on salads, soups, and sandwiches. My favorite way to serve it as a dipper with crusty bread pieces and chunks of cheeses on a charcuterie board.

> 1 cup extra virgin olive oil
> ½ tsp. dried oregano
> ½ tsp. Hatch red or green chile powder (Hatch Chile Marketplace, 175)
> 2 cloves fresh garlic, minced
> 1 tsp. crushed red pepper flakes
> ½ tsp. Italian seasoning
> ½ tsp. sea salt

1. Combine all ingredients in a small bowl. Stir occasionally until blended well.
2. Serve immediately or transfer to an airtight container and store in a cool place for up to 2 days.

Variation: Add 3 tbsp. balsamic vinegar for a more intense flavor combination.

HATCH GREEN CHILE CREAM SAUCE

MAKES 2 CUPS

Sauces like this are keepers: easy, light, and flavorful. I have poured this over a pan of chicken enchiladas before baking, served it fresh over crispy rolled tacos, or offered it as a dipper on a charcuterie tray. Warm or cold, this sauce is delicious.

> 2 cups Hatch green chile, roasted, peeled, seeded, and minced
> 3 cloves fresh garlic, minced
> 1 cup heavy cream
> 1 tsp. kosher salt

1. Combine chile, garlic, and cream in a food processor or blender and pulse or blend for 1 to 2 minutes until smooth.
2. Add salt and pulse until well blended or about 30 seconds. Transfer to an airtight container and refrigerate for 2 to 3 days.

HATCH ASIAN SAUCE

MAKES 1 ¼ CUP

This tasty sauce is good for dipping—I love it for dipping my Hatch Chile Spring Rolls and Hatch Chile Wontons. But I also drizzle it over salads and sandwiches. Sweet, spicy, and savory, it is also delicious on grilled chicken.

½ cup granulated sugar
2 tbsp. cornstarch
1 tsp. Hatch red chile powder (Hatch Chile Marketplace, 175)
⅔ cup water
½ cup soy sauce
⅓ cup red wine vinegar
1 tbsp. ketchup
1 tsp. hot pepper flakes

1. In a small bowl, combine sugar, cornstarch, and chile powder.

2. In a saucepan, combine water, soy sauce, vinegar, ketchup, and hot pepper flakes over medium-high heat.

3. Slowly add sugar mixture, mixing well. Bring to a boil. Reduce heat to medium low and boil gently, stirring, until sauce thickens, 4 to 6 minutes. Let sauce cool. Serve immediately or transfer to an airtight container or squeeze bottle and refrigerate, stirring occasionally, for up to 4 days.

HATCH MEXICAN WHITE SAUCE

MAKES 1 CUP

I often use this sauce for a final zest of flavor. I discovered this little accent sauce years ago in San Diego served on fish tacos . . . so good! My version has a bit more spice and flavor.

> ¾ cup mayonnaise
> ½ cup plain yogurt
> Juice of 1 lime
> 1 tsp. Hatch green chile powder (Hatch Chile Marketplace, 175)*
> ½ tsp. minced cilantro

1. In a medium bowl, combine mayonnaise and yogurt. Add lime juice and whisk until smooth.

2. Add chile powder and cilantro and blend well.

3. Refrigerate for up to 1 hour. Transfer to an airtight container or squeeze bottle.

4. When using this sauce for decorative garnish, place it in a squeeze bottle and drizzle over tacos, enchiladas, burritos, or queso.

* Substitute 1 tsp. of Hatch red chile powder for the Hatch green chile powder.

(*left to right*) Hatch Chile Salsa Verde, Hatch Chile Come Back Sauce, Chile Avocado Sauce, and Hatch Chile and Lime Mayo.

HATCH CHIMICHURRI

MAKES 2 CUPS

Fresh herbs complement the flavors of Hatch green chile in this condiment. Originating in Argentina, chimichurri is a loose oil-based sauce created with fresh greens to accent grilled meats. Add a drizzle over grilled steak or a dollop in a soup or stew to elevate the flavor with freshness and heat.

2 cups chopped fresh cilantro
1 ½ cups chopped flat-leaf parsley
3 green onions, ends removed, green parts only, chopped
⅓ cup Hatch green chile, roasted, seeded, peeled, and chopped
4 cloves garlic, minced
½ cup olive oil
Juice of 2 to 3 limes
Kosher salt
Freshly ground black pepper

1. Wash and rinse your greens well and pat dry.

2. In a food processor, pulse together cilantro, parsley, green onions, chile, garlic, oil, and lime juice until smooth and well blended.

3. Season with salt and pepper to taste.

4. Serve immediately at room temperature or transfer to an airtight container and refrigerate for 1 hour or for up to 2 to 3 days. Bring to room temperature before serving.

CHILE MUSTARD

MAKES 1 CUP

Chile mustard! This is for all my mustard-loving friends. A simple spread for hamburgers, hotdogs, or Sonoran hot dogs, or a great dipper for pretzels and crackers. The tanginess of the pickles adds a tart element to the heat of the chile.

> ¾ cup Hatch green chile, roasted, peeled, seeded, and chopped
> ¼ cup chopped dill pickle
> 1 clove garlic minced
> 1 cup prepared mustard

1. In a medium bowl, gently combine chile, pickles, and garlic.
2. Fold in mustard and mix well. Serve immediately or transfer to an airtight container and refrigerate for up to 1 week.

WHIPPED BLUE CHEESE AND CHILE CREAM

MAKES 1 CUP

If you like a good smear on a bagel or a burger, this cream is for you. I love to smear it on bagels or cocktail crackers, and occasionally I will top a baked potato with a dollop. The chile-cheese combination is unique but flavorful.

> One 8-oz. package of cream cheese, softened
> 4 oz. blue cheese, crumbled
> 2 tbsp. whipping cream
> 1 tbsp. olive oil
> 1 tsp. cracked black pepper
> Pinch of kosher salt
> 2 tbsp. Hatch green chile, roasted, peeled, and minced

1. In a food processor, combine cream cheese, blue cheese, whipping cream, olive oil, and pepper until smooth.
2. Transfer cream sauce to a medium bowl and gently fold in salt and minced green chile, mixing well. Transfer to an airtight container and refrigerate for 1 hour or up to 2 to 3 days.

HATCH CHILE COME BACK SAUCE

MAKES ¾ CUP

Come back Sauce is a southern favorite, with its name originating from the traditional goodbye in the South, encouraging all to "come back" soon. My version adds a bit of heat and southwestern hospitality—so "Come Back" soon and get more chile!

> ½ cup mayonnaise
> 2 tbsp. ketchup
> 1 tsp. Worcestershire sauce
> ½ tsp. Hatch extra hot red chile powder (Hatch Chile Marketplace, 175)
> ½ tsp. garlic powder

1. In a medium bowl, combine mayonnaise, ketchup, Worcestershire sauce, chile powder, and garlic powder. Blend until smooth.

2. Transfer to an airtight container and refrigerate for 1 hour or up to 2 to 3 days.

(opposite page, clockwise) Hatch Green Taco Sauce, Chile Avocado Salsa, Spicy Veggie Salsa, Hatch Chile Comeback Sauce, Chile Mustard, Hatch Green Sauce, Pickled Hatch Green Chile, Hatch Red Chile Sauce *(center)*.

HATCH CHILE ASSOCIATION

The Hatch Chile Association was created in 2014. According to Duane Gillis, the current president, "A group of growers here in the valley wanted to protect and promote the growing, processing, and marketing of Hatch chile." That is their mission. There has been an increase in chile grown outside of the valley using the Hatch name. The vision was to create an easy authentication for products made with Hatch chile through the use of the association's certified Hatch logo. The association's values focus on honesty and truth in labeling. Its members are committed to protecting authentic Hatch chile products.

So look for the Certified Hatch chile logo!

www.certifiedhatch.com

HATCH CHILE AND LIME MAYO

MAKES 1 CUP

This mayonnaise is simple yet perfect on a turkey or ham sandwich and fabulous on a Mexican Torta sandwich. Crown a filet of fish with this rich mayo laced with lime for an elegant entrée (See my Hatch Halibut, 227).

> 1 cup mayonnaise
> 1 tbsp. fresh lime juice
> 1 tsp. Hatch green chile powder (Hatch Chile Marketplace, 175)
> ¼ cup hot Hatch green chile, roasted, peeled, seeded, and minced

1. In a small bowl, combine mayonnaise, lime juice, chile powder, and minced green chile. Mix well.

2. Serve immediately or transfer to an airtight container and refrigerate for up to 1 week.

RED CHILE MOLE

MAKES 2 ½ CUPS

Mole is savory-sweet, elegant, flavorful sauce that is versatile and easy to prepare. It can transform a baked chicken, elevate enchiladas to a different level of flavor, and give a nice finish to a grilled rack of ribs. Garnishes such as minced pecans, shallots, or sesame seeds complement this sauce nicely.

> ¼ cup chicken broth
> 1 tsp. hot pepper flakes
> ½ tsp. dried oregano
> 1 tsp. ground cumin
> ½ tsp. garlic powder
> 1 tsp. onion powder
> 2 cups Hatch Red Chile Sauce (112)
> 2 oz. semisweet chocolate, chopped into small pieces

1. In a saucepan, combine broth, pepper flakes, oregano, cumin, garlic powder, and onion powder over medium heat for 1 to 2 minutes, whisking spices together. Add chile sauce, stirring, until well blended, 3 to 5 minutes.

2. Reduce heat to low and add chocolate. Stir until chocolate is melted. Remove from heat and cool. Serve immediately or let cool to room temperature. Transfer to an airtight container and refrigerate for up to 1 week.

CHEESY GREEN CHILE SAUCE

MAKES 2 CUPS

Warm, cheesy, and rich, this sauce does not disappoint. This cheesy fiery goodness is almost like a queso and crowns our beloved burritos and enchiladas like an enchilada sauce. A pinch of cumin adds that Tex Mex flavor, which I like from time to time.

  1 tbsp. butter
  ½ cup Hatch green chile, roasted, peeled, seeded, and chopped
  ½ cup chicken broth
  1 cup heavy cream
  1 cup cheddar cheese, grated
  1 cup Monterey Jack cheese
  ¼ tsp. cumin (optional)

1. In a skillet sauté butter and chile over medium heat for 1 to 2 minutes.

2. Add broth and cream, stirring frequently until heated through, about 2 to 3 minutes.

3. Reduce heat to low and slowly add cheese and cumin. Stir while cheese melts.

4. Serve immediately or let cool to room temperature.

5. Transfer to a resealable container and refrigerate for up to 1 week.

HATCH RED CHILE SAUCE

MAKES 2 CUPS

As the August harvest progresses to early fall, the chiles start to turn red. The spicy flavor of green chile gives way to the earthiness and rich flavor of red chile. This authentic sauce is made from dried red chiles. It is a time-consuming process but worth the effort.

> 8 dried New Mexico red chile peppers, destemmed and seeded
> Water
> 6 tbsp. vegetable oil, divided
> 5 cloves garlic, minced
> 2 tbsp. all-purpose flour
> Kosher salt to taste

1. To soften the chiles, place them in a bowl and cover with about 1 quart of water. Chill or refrigerate for at least 10 hours.

2. Drain liquid from chiles and set aside. In a blender, puree softened chiles with 1 ½ cups reserved liquid until smooth. Puree should be thick but pourable. Add additional soaking liquid if needed.

3. Press chile puree through a fine-mesh sieve or a strainer, discarding remaining skin and seeds. Place puree in a bowl and set aside.

4. In a large skillet, heat 2 tbsp. of oil over medium heat. Add garlic and sauté until soft, about 1 minute, then add chile puree. Bring to a gentle boil. Reduce heat to low and simmer, stirring occasionally, until flavors are well blended, 8 to 10 minutes. Remove from heat.

5. In a small bowl, add remaining oil. Gradually stir in flour, creating a roux (a thick paste).

6. Return skillet with red sauce to burner and increase heat to medium. Gradually stir roux into chile sauce, about 1 tsp. at a time, stirring constantly.

7. Reduce heat and simmer, adding salt 1 tsp. at a time, tasting as you continue stirring, until thick and smooth, 6 to 8 minutes. Serve immediately or let cool to room temperature. Transfer to an airtight container and refrigerate for up to 3 days.

Variations:

When I am pressed for time I use prepared Hatch red chile puree (Hatch Chile
Marketplace, 175); omit dried red chile pods and water, then follow the rest of the
recipe as directed.

Fresh Red Chile Version (photo on page 107): Using fresh red chile that has not gone
through the drying process creates a more textured, sweeter sauce. Omit dried
red chile peppers and add 8 fresh red chile chiles, roasted, peeled, seeded, and
chopped. Skip steps 1, 2, and 3, and instead place chiles in blender and pulse for 2
minutes. Continue with steps 4, 5 and 6.

HATCH GREEN CHILE SAUCE

MAKES 2 CUPS

The essence of our Mexican-style sauces is our Hatch Green Chile Sauce. Loaded with natural chile flavor, this sauce is perfect for smothering enchiladas, burritos, eggs, and grilled favorites.

3 tbsp. olive oil, divided
2 cloves garlic, minced
1 onion, diced
2 cups Hatch green chile, roasted, peeled, seeded, and chopped
1 cup chicken or vegetable broth
¼ cup all-purpose flour

1. In a large skillet, sauté garlic, onion, and chile in 1 tbsp. oil until onion is transparent, about 3 to 4 minutes. Add broth and bring to a boil over medium-high heat. Reduce heat and bring to a gentle boil, about 4 to 6 minutes.

2. In a small bowl, combine flour and remaining 2 tbsp. oil, blending well to create a roux (a thick paste).

3. Gradually stir roux into chile sauce, 1 tsp. at a time, over medium heat, whisking until smooth and thick, 6 to 8 minutes. Serve immediately or let cool to room temperature. Transfer to an airtight container and refrigerate for up to 2 days.

Variation: Elevate flavor by adding 1 tomato, seeded and diced, in step 1.

GREEN CHILE WINE SAUCE

MAKES 1 ½ CUPS

As I have said, green chile goes with everything—even wine! This is such a favorite sauce in our house, I keep it on hand for a light drizzle here and there. White wine blends well with green chile, creating a unique flavor.

> ½ cup minced green onions
> 1 cup low-sodium chicken broth
> ½ cup white wine
> 3 tbsp. white vinegar
> ½ cup Hatch green chile, roasted, peeled, seeded, and mashed or pureed
> 4 tbsp. butter

1. Coat a medium-sized skillet with cooking spray and sauté onions until they start to soften, about 2 minutes. Add broth, wine, vinegar, and chile and bring to a boil.

2. Remove from heat and stir in butter until melted and well blended. Serve immediately or cool and transfer to an airtight container and refrigerate for up to 1 week.

RED CHILE WINE SAUCE

MAKES 2 CUPS

This rich wine sauce has a hint of chile that complements pasta, grilled or roasted beef, and so much more. Red wine complements red chile, so creating a rich red sauce was an obvious next step.

    4 tbsp. unsalted butter
    2 to 3 large shallots
    1 ¼ cup red wine
    2 ½ cups beef broth
    ⅓ cup Hatch Red Chile Puree (117, or Hatch Chile Marketplace, 175)
    Kosher salt
    Ground black pepper
    1 tsp. sugar
    2 tbsp. all-purpose flour
    2 tbsp. salted butter, melted

1. In a medium pot, sauté unsalted butter and shallots until soft and translucent, about 3 to 5 minutes.

2. Add the wine, broth, and red chile puree. Bring to a boil and cook over medium heat for about 30 minutes, until liquid is reduced in volume.

3. While liquid is reducing, combine salt and pepper, sugar, flour, and salted melted butter in a small bowl.

4. Once wine mixture is reduced, reduce heat to medium low. Slowly whisk in flour mixture, stirring constantly.

5. Simmer for a few minutes, until sauce is thickened. Serve immediately or cool and transfer to an airtight container and refrigerate for up to 3 days.

HATCH RED CHILE PUREE

MAKES 2 CUPS

This is our way of making a seasonal delight into a year-round addiction. This is the foundation for wonderful, authentic Hatch red chile recipes. Taking the time to process dried red chile into a puree will pay off for months to come.

6 to 8 dried New Mexico red chile peppers
4 cloves fresh garlic, chopped
Water

1. Destem and shake the seeds out of each chile.

2. Place chiles in a large pot and cover them with water. Boil until chiles are soft and hydrated, about 20 minutes. Remove chiles from the pot with tongs and place in a bowl. Reserve liquid from pot.

3. In a blender or food processor, puree chiles and garlic with 1 ½ cups reserved liquid until smooth. Puree should be thick but pourable. Add additional liquid if needed.

4. Press chile puree through a fine-mesh sieve or a strainer into a large bowl, mashing chile with a spoon or muddling tool to create puree. Discard skin and seeds.

5. Use immediately or transfer chile puree to an airtight container and refrigerate up to 3 days or place in freezer for up to 3 months.

SWEET CARAMEL CHILE SAUCE

MAKES 1 CUP

This caramel chile–laced sauce is so versatile. Rich caramel accented with red chile is smooth but sweet. Drizzle it over a slice of apple pie or ice cream.

> 1 cup brown sugar
> 1 tsp. Hatch hot red chile powder (Hatch Chile Marketplace, 175)
> ½ cup butter
> ½ cup half-and-half cream
> Dash of vanilla extract

1. In a small bowl, combine sugar and chile until well blended.

2. In a saucepan, melt butter and add half-and-half over medium-low heat. Add sugar mixture.

3. Cook over medium-high heat, bringing to a boil, while stirring until sugar is completely dissolved, about 5 to 7 minutes.

4. Remove from heat and whisk in vanilla extract and mix well. Serve immediately or cool to room temperature and transfer to an airtight container and refrigerate for up to 1 week.

HATCH CHILE RASPBERRY SAUCE

MAKES 1 ½ CUPS

Now that raspberries are so plentiful these days, I find myself craving them more than ever! This special sauce is a flavorful surprise of fruit and chile. Serve over Brie or cream cheese for happy hour or drizzle over pancakes and waffles for an amazing breakfast.

> 2 cups fresh raspberries
> 1 ¾ cup water
> ⅓ cup of sugar
> 1 tsp. lemon juice
> 1 tbsp. water
> 2 tbsp. corn starch
> ⅓ cup Hatch green chile, roasted, peeled, seeded, and chopped

1. In a medium saucepan, combine raspberries, water, and sugar over medium heat. Stir constantly, bringing to a boil. Reduce heat and simmer for 20 minutes. Remove from heat.

2. Carefully mash sauce through a strainer into a medium bowl, catching the seeds and discarding them.

3. Return sauce to saucepan over medium-low heat. Add lemon juice and stir.

4. In a small bowl combine water and cornstarch. Slowly add to raspberry sauce, stirring constantly until sauce thickens, about 2 to 3 minutes.

5. Fold in green chile, blending well. Remove from heat and serve immediately or cool to room temperature and transfer to an airtight container and refrigerate for up to 3 days.

QUICK RASPBERRY SAUCE

MAKES 1 CUP

1 cup seedless raspberry jam
½ cup Hatch green chile, roasted, peeled, seeded, and chopped
Pinch of kosher salt

1. In a small saucepan, heat jam over medium-low heat.

2. Once jam is heated through, add chile and salt. Increase heat to medium, stirring until well blended, about 2 to 3 minutes. Remove from heat and let cool to room temperature. Serve immediately or transfer to an airtight container and refrigerate for up to 3 days.

HATCH ROSEMARY SALT

MAKES 1 CUP

This nicely flavored salt with a hint of chile is perfect for steak, chicken, or even on pizza. The flavor of fresh rosemary and ground chile engages the senses and tastes wonderful. I tend to throw a dash of this on a lot of entrées and salads!

¾ cup kosher salt
¼ cup sea salt
2 tbsp. fresh rosemary, minced
1 tbsp. dried green chile powder (Hatch Chile Marketplace, 175)

1. Combine salts, rosemary, and chile powder in a medium bowl. Mix until well blended.

2. Transfer to an airtight container. Let flavored salt stand overnight before using.

HATCH RED CHILE SALT

MAKES ¼ CUP

A fine-grain sea salt blend with earthy chile and citrus flavors creates a perfect seasoning for pastas, sandwiches, soups, and salads. I often use this seasoning to salt the rim of a margarita or my Hatchelada. This flavor combination is simple but delicious.

> ¼ cup pink Himalayan salt
> 1 tsp. Hatch red chile powder (Hatch Chile Marketplace, 175)
> 1 tsp. lime-flavored salt*

1. In a small bowl combine salt and chile powder and blend well. Store in an airtight container. Transfer to an airtight container and store at room temperature.

* Lime-flavored salt has a tangy citrus flavor and can be found at your local market or online.

HATCH RED CHILE RUB

MAKES ¼ CUP

Rub this red chile spice on meats and chicken to add a layer of memorable flavor that is sweet and savory. Once cooked it creates a nice crusty texture on the surface, so use it liberally. I love it on chicken wings, rib eye steak, and seared salmon.

> 2 tbsp. brown sugar
> 1 tsp. Hatch hot red chile powder (Hatch Chile Marketplace, 175)
> ½ tsp. granulated garlic
> 1 tsp. pink Himalayan salt*

1. In a small bowl, combine sugar, chile powder, garlic, and salt and mix well. Transfer to an airtight container and store at room temperature.

* 1 tsp. kosher salt can be substituted for pink Himalayan salt for a slightly different flavor.

4 SALADS AND SIDES

THE FIELDS OF PRODUCE IN THE Hatch Valley are bursting with abundance. Harvests throughout the year yield crops of onions, corn, squash, lettuce, watermelon, cabbage, and pinto beans. This collection of recipes was created with the best seasonal produce from Hatch in mind. You can shop at your local markets, farmers markets, and microfarms for the freshest items. However, you will find fresh and distinct flavor combinations in these recipes regardless of where you source your ingredients. The Hatch Cobb Salad is served platter-style and is great for a crowd. The Baked Squash and Chile is pure comfort food, a perfect side for grilled chicken or roasted pork loin. Red Chile Sweet Potatoes and Green Chile Holiday Dressing will add fun and flavor to your holiday meals.

Complementing a main dish with fresh and tasty sides adds a balance of flavor, and Hatch chile adds a bit of excitement and surprise to any meal. These dishes are nutrient-driven and pack a lot of freshness and goodness in a single serving. Serve some of these favorites as vegetarian entrées, like my Mexican Street Salad.

125

Finally, I have to say I am not a baker, so simplicity in making homemade bread is a must for me. These recipes are simple and straightforward; they take some time but are so worth it. My Green Chile Cheese Bread, a simple yeast bread, is packed with flavor. The Green Chile Scones make quite a statement as well, served with breakfast or alongside a bowl of Hatch Green Chile Stew. All of these are mindful and delicious recipes that reflect the abundance of produce often found in the Hatch Valley.

(*opposite page*) Freshly harvested Hatch fresh red chile at the Chile Express in Hatch.

MEXICAN STREET SALAD

MAKES 4 TO 6 SERVINGS

If you're looking to find the ultimate street food south of the border, this dish brings it home. Charred corn and roasted green chile blended with citrus offers a smokey, spicy, and tangy experience. This salad recipe is full of color and flavor and can be served as a main entrée or side dish. Try it as a tasty garnish on enchiladas and grilled burgers.

½ cup freshly squeezed lime juice
⅓ cup olive oil
1 tsp. cumin
2 cloves garlic, minced
2 cups whole corn kernels*
2 tbsp. honey
3 Hatch green chiles, roasted, peeled, seeded, and chopped
¼ cup of cilantro, chopped
10 grape tomatoes, sliced in half
½ cup cotija cheese, crumbled
1 lime, cut in wedges

1. In a small bowl combine lime juice, olive oil, cumin, garlic, and honey. Whisk until well blended. Set aside.

2. In a large skillet, cook corn over medium-high heat, until corn starts to char up, about 10 to 12 minutes. Remove from heat and cool to room temperature.

3. In a large bowl, combine corn, green chile, cilantro, and tomatoes. Mix well.

4. Drizzle corn mixture with dressing and toss gently. Chill for 1 hour. Before serving, garnish with cheese and lime wedges.

Variation: For a larger salad, place 6 cups of chopped romaine lettuce or fresh greens on a serving platter. Top with corn mixture, gently toss, and serve immediately.
* You can shuck 2 ears of corn, which will yield about 2 cups of corn, then toss into boiling water for 3 minutes and drain. But if I am pressed for time I use drained canned corn or thawed frozen corn.

HATCH CHILE CHICKEN SALAD

MAKES 4 SERVINGS

Chicken salad is more than just a family favorite: you can turn it into a delicious filling by adding a bit of spice. Fresh green chile gives this recipe a distinctive flavor with a balance of traditional creaminess and crunch. It is perfect in a chicken salad sandwich, served on a bed of lettuce, or as a spread for crackers or celery stalks.

> 2 cups cooked chicken, shredded
> ½ cup green chile, roasted, peeled, seeded, and chopped
> 1 stalk celery, chopped
> 1 green onion, chopped
> ½ cup mayonnaise
> ½ tsp. mustard
> ½ tsp. fresh lime juice
> 1 tsp. salt

1. In a medium bowl, combine chicken, green chile, celery, and onion.

2. Gently fold in mayonnaise, mustard, lime juice, and salt until well mixed.

3. Refrigerate for up to 1 hour until chilled through or transfer to an airtight container and refrigerate for up to 2 days.

MORROW FARMS

In 1940 W. H. Mundy (Pop) moved his family from Las Cruces, New Mexico, to the Hatch Valley. The family grew cotton and alfalfa. W. H. was also a "great earth mover," according to some. He did dirt work on the Caballo Dam, helping to create Caballo Lake, as well as on the canal system in nearby Las Cruces.

In 1965 W. H.'s grandson, Joe Morrow, who had grown up on the farm but was living in Arizona, returned to Hatch and took over the family farm. He and his boys John and Harvey expanded the operation, planting onions in 1975 and chile in 1981 in the Rincon area near Hatch. They grew Sandia and other varieties of chile and had contracts with Joy Canning, Mountain Pass, Bueno, and Ashley Foods. In 2021 Morrow Farms was named Hatch Chile Festival Farmer of the year.

Today, Morrow Farms has expanded into the neighboring Uves Valley, growing onions, pinto beans, watermelon, corn, hay, and Hatch chile—green and red. The Morrow family celebrates four generations of family living and working in the valley. Laura, John's wife, shared that during the winter months the family always enjoys their rich red chile sauce on enchiladas, eggs, and steak. But they are sure to put fresh-roasted Hatch green chile on everything else year-round!

Chile harvest, late August 2021, with John Morrow and his wife, Dr. Laura Boyd.

HATCH COBB SALAD

I enjoy the rich textures and flavor of a good cobb salad: the chicken, bacon, blue cheese, egg, and avocado. Adding a Hatch green chile and a spicy chile vinaigrette elevates the taste of this American favorite.

    6 cups chopped romaine lettuce
    2 cups Hatch green chile, roasted, peeled, seeded, and chopped*
    8 slices bacon, cooked and crumbled
    1 chicken breast, grilled and chopped
    1 medium red onion, thinly sliced
    1 cup blue cheese, crumbled
    1 avocado, peeled, seeded, and diced
    2 eggs, hard boiled and quartered
    10 grape tomatoes, each cut in half
    Green or Red Hatch Chile Vinaigrette (97)

1. Arrange lettuce on a large serving platter. Place chile and bacon in the middle of the platter.

2. Divide chicken and place on either side of chile and bacon.

3. Divide onion, blue cheese, avocado, eggs, and tomatoes and place on opposite sides of the platter around the edges.

4. Refrigerate for up to 1 hour until chilled through. Serve with vinaigrette.

* Using a mild green chile keeps the heat from overpowering the elements of this salad.

BAKED SQUASH AND CHILE

MAKES 6 SERVINGS

This baked vegetable casserole is loaded with flavor. Hatch green chile is tucked among layers of fresh squash and creamy cheese. I love how the buttered bread crumbs give this dish a crispy finish.

- 2 medium onions, thinly sliced
- 2 tbsp. butter, divided
- 1 tbsp. olive oil
- 3 to 4 medium zucchini, sliced and cut into ¼-inch pieces
- 3 to 4 medium yellow squash, sliced and cut into ¼-inch pieces
- ½ cup sour cream
- 1 cup Hatch green chile, roasted, peeled, seeded, and chopped
- 1 ½ cups Monterey Jack cheese, shredded
- 2 cloves garlic, minced
- 1 tbsp. fresh Italian parsley, minced
- 3 tbsp. bread crumbs
- 2 tbsp. Parmesan cheese

1. Preheat oven to 350 degrees. Prepare a medium-sized baking pan with cooking spray.

2. In a large skillet, sauté onions and garlic in 1 tbsp. butter and olive oil over medium heat until soft, 3 to 5 minutes. Add zucchini and squash and cook until soft but firm, 5 to 8 minutes. Remove from heat and gently fold in sour cream until well blended.

3. Spread onion squash mixture evenly across the bottom of the baking pan. Top with a layer of chile and cheese.

4. In a small bowl, combine parsley, bread crumbs, and Parmesan cheese. Add remaining butter (melted) and mix well.

5. Top squash mixture with bread crumbs, spreading evenly across the top.

6. Bake until bubbly and lightly browned, about 20 minutes. Serve immediately.

GREEN CHILE HOLIDAY DRESSING/STUFFING

MAKES 6 SERVINGS

Our family loves Thanksgiving dinner. It is the typical traditional fare with turkey, dressing, and mashed potatoes. Some years back I decided to add Hatch chile to my dressing. It was a hit and is now requested every year. Some years I add spicy sausage, but I always make it with chile.

> ½ cup unsalted butter
> 2 cups onion
> 3 cups celery
> 1 tsp. dried sage
> 1 tsp. flat leaf parsley
> 1 tsp. minced fresh rosemary
> 1 cup hot Hatch green chile, roasted, peeled, seeded, and chopped
> 10 to 12 cups bread pieces*
> 3 to 4 cups chicken, poultry, or vegetable stock (low sodium)

1. Preheat oven to 350 degrees. Melt butter in a large skillet, add onion and celery, and cook until soft and translucent. Add sage, parsley, rosemary, and green chile. Mix well.

2. Place bread pieces in a large bowl and gently add onion mixture. Fold gently until all ingredients are well blended. Add stock and blend well until moist.

3. Transfer to a well-greased 9 × 13 in. casserole dish. Cover with foil. Bake for 20 to 30 minutes until heated through. Serve immediately.

* This number of bread pieces equals about 1.5 loaves of bread. You can mix stale and fresh bread for this recipe. I recommend a mixture of white, wheat, or French bread. You can even try sourdough bread for extra flavor.

HATCH CHILE RICE

MAKES 4 TO 6 SERVINGS

I have made this rice for years. It is similar to Spanish rice, but the red chile puree sets it apart. Garlic, onion, tomato, and chile accent the rice and create a light, easy side dish. This side dish complements Mexican entrées of grilled chicken, steak, or shrimp.

2 tbsp. vegetable oil
3 cloves garlic, minced
1 ¼ cup long-grain white rice
¾ cup tomato sauce
¼ cup Hatch Red Chile Puree (117, or Hatch Chile Marketplace, 175)
3 cups water
½ tsp. salt

1. In a large skillet, heat oil over medium heat. Sauté garlic until soft, about 1 minute. Add rice, stirring as it browns slightly, 4 to 6 minutes.

2. Add tomato sauce, chile puree, water, and salt. Blend well.

3. Bring to a boil. Cover and simmer on medium low until rice is tender and liquid has evaporated, about 15 to 20 minutes.

4. Fluff rice, then transfer to a serving bowl.

Variation: For green chile rice, omit tomato sauce and red chile puree. Replace with 1 cup Hatch green chile that has been pureed in a food processor with 3 tbsp. water.

HATCH CHILE MAC AND CHEESE

MAKES 6 SERVINGS

This casserole-style dish is a show stealer! A thick and creamy sauce envelops the pasta while fresh-roasted green chile adds heat and texture. As our culinary palates become adventurous, we welcome these nuanced changes to our traditional favorites.

4 cups dried elbow macaroni
¼ cup butter
¼ cup flour
1 cup heavy cream
1 cup whole milk
2 tsp. dry mustard
1 egg, beaten
3 cups sharp cheddar cheese, divided
1 ½ cups Hatch green chile, roasted, peeled, and chopped
1 tsp. salt
½ tsp. ground black pepper
1 tbsp fresh flat parsley, minced

1. Preheat oven to 325 degrees. Meanwhile, cook macaroni as directed on the package. Do not overcook. Drain and set aside.

2. In a saucepan, melt butter over medium-low heat. Add flour and whisk until well blended, about 3 to 4 minutes. Slowly add cream, milk, and mustard. Cool for 3 to 5 minutes.

3. In a small bowl, very slowly add about ½ cup of sauce to the whisked egg, whisking the mixture so the egg does not cook. Then slowly incorporate the egg mixture into the sauce, stirring slowly.

4. Add 2 ½ cups of cheese and green chile into the sauce and stir until melted, then add salt and pepper.

5. Pour over drained macaroni and gently mix until macaroni is well coated.

6. Pour macaroni mixture into a well-greased 7 × 11 in. baking dish and top with remaining cheese.

7. Place dish in oven and bake for 20 to 25 minutes, until bubbly and cheese is melted. Garnish with parsley and serve immediately.

Variation: For a creamier version, process the green chile in a food processor until smooth, about 3 to 4 minutes. Combine as directed. Top macaroni mixture with an additional 1 cup of grated Monterey Jack cheese after pouring macaroni into well-greased pan. Bake as instructed.

HATCH SCALLOPED SKILLET POTATOES

MAKES 4 TO 6 SERVINGS

I love potatoes . . . mashed, fried, baked, it does not matter. But scalloped potatoes laced with Hatch green chile take the prize! They are cheesy, creamy, crunchy, and delicious. Pair with a favorite meat or chicken entrée.

4 tbsp. butter
3 Hatch green chiles, roasted, peeled, seeded, and chopped
½ cup minced green onions
2 garlic cloves, minced
2 tsp. salt
2 tsp. cracked black pepper
1 ½ cups heavy cream
1 cup half-and-half cream
2 cups cheddar cheese, grated
2 cups Monterey Jack cheese, grated
4 to 6 medium potatoes, cut into 1/16-inch-thick slices

1. In a medium saucepan melt butter and sauté chile, onion, garlic, salt, and pepper over medium heat, about 4 to 5 minutes.

2. Add cream and half-and-half, reduce heat, and simmer until heated through. Slowly add cheeses, stirring until cheese is melted and well blended.

3. Place potato slices in a lightly greased 8-inch iron skillet, creating a ring around the outer edges and moving inward. Fill the entire skillet, placing slices close together.

4. Slowly pour cream mixture over the potatoes.

5. Place skillet on a baking sheet in case of bubbling over. Bake, covered with foil, for 30 minutes at 400 degrees. Then reduce heat to 350 degrees and bake for 50 minutes. Serve immediately.

GREEN CHILE MASHED POTATOES

MAKES 4 SERVINGS

Hatch chile takes these mashed potatoes from good to great. By adding a chile paste to these mashed potatoes I created a new side dish that will become a favorite.

> 1 ½ cups Hatch green chile, roasted, peeled, seeded, and chopped
> 6 garlic cloves, peeled and chopped
> ½ cup olive oil
> 4 to 5 medium baking potatoes, peeled and cut into 1-inch cubes
> ¼ cup butter
> ½ cup milk, warmed
> 4 oz. cream cheese, softened
> Kosher salt

1. Place chile and garlic in a food processor and pulse on low while slowly adding olive oil.

2. Pulse chile mixture until smooth. Set aside.

3. Fill a large pot half full of water and bring to a boil over medium-high heat. Add potato cubes and boil until tender, about 18 to 20 minutes. Drain water from pot.

4. Place potatoes, butter, milk, and cream cheese into an electric stand mixer and mix with paddle attachment until well blended.

5. Slowly add chile mixture and salt to taste.

RED CHILE SWEET POTATOES

Perfectly baked sweet potatoes are no fuss and easy. Adding a slather of red chile sauce and caramelized onions makes them memorable. The red chile and sweetness of these potatoes is accented with a bit of ginger.

> 4 sweet potatoes, scrubbed and clean
> 2 tbsp. olive oil
> 3 onions, thinly sliced
> 1 clove garlic, minced
> ½ tsp. fresh ginger, finely grated
> 1 ½ tsp. salt, divided
> 4 tbsp. butter, divided
> ⅓ cup Hatch Red Chile Sauce (112), warmed

1. Preheat oven to 425 degrees. Prick the potatoes and place on a lined baking sheet.

2. Bake until tender, about 50 minutes.

3. While potatoes are baking, pour oil in a large skillet. Add onions, garlic, and ginger. Sauté covered over medium-high heat, stirring constantly. As onions turn brown, add ¾ tsp. salt and continue to stir as they caramelize, about 30 to 50 minutes .

4. Remove potatoes from oven and slice open the top of each potato. Place 1 tbsp. butter on top of each potato, fluffing the center of each with a fork, and sprinkle with remaining salt.

5. Spoon 1 tbsp. red chile sauce on top of each potato and top with caramelized onions. Serve immediately.

LOADED HATCH BAKED POTATOES

MAKES 4 SERVINGS

These spuds are filled with savory goodness. A crispy-skinned potato with a fluffy, pillowy center is irresistible, especially when it is laced with Hatch chile. A loaded baked potato pairs well with meats and chicken and can even make a meal in itself.

  2 large russet baking potatoes
  Olive oil
  Kosher salt
  4 tbsp. butter, divided
  1 cup sour cream
  Salt and pepper
  6 slices bacon, cooked and crumbled
  4 green onions, minced
  1 cup Hatch green chile, roasted, peeled, seeded, and chopped
  1½ cups cheddar cheese, grated
  1 tsp. Hatch red chile powder (Hatch Chile Marketplace, 175)

1. Preheat oven to 400 degrees.

2. Wash and dry potatoes. Poke both potatoes several times and rub with olive oil and sprinkle with kosher salt.

3. Place on the center rack and bake until soft in the middle, about 1 hour. Check with a sharp knife to see if they are soft through the center.

4. Remove potatoes from oven and allow to cool slightly. Reduce heat to 200 degrees.

5. Slice each potato lengthwise and place four sides on a baking sheet or platter.

6. Using a fork, fluff the potato centers while adding 1 tbsp. butter and a scoop of sour cream on each. Season with salt and pepper.

7. Once the butter and sour cream have melted on each potato half, fluff again.

8. Top each potato half evenly with bacon, onion, and chile, then top each potato half with equal amounts of cheese and red chile powder.

9. Place in oven for 10 to 12 minutes until cheese has melted and potatoes are heated through. Serve immediately.

HATCH POTATO SALAD

A classic potato salad with a southwestern twist creates a new side that you will add to your recipe list. Adding cumin to the mayonnaise sauce and fresh green chile brings this chilled salad to a new level with a southwestern flavor.

> 6 medium Yukon gold potatoes, peeled, cubed, and boiled until soft but firm
> 6 green onions, chopped
> 2 celery stalks, diced
> 1 cup Hatch green chile, roasted, peeled, seeded, and chopped
> ½ cup diced sweet pickles, drained; reserve 2 tbsp. pickle juice
> 1 ½ cups mayonnaise
> ¼ cup mustard
> ½ tsp. cumin
> ¾ tsp. salt
> ¼ tsp. ground black pepper
> 4 hard-boiled eggs, diced

1. Place potatoes in a large bowl and allow to cool. Add onions, celery, green chile, and pickles. Toss together until well blended.

2. In a smaller bowl, combine mayonnaise, mustard, reserved pickle juice, cumin, salt, and pepper and mix well. Gently fold mixture into the potatoes until well coated with sauce.

3. Gently add hard-boiled eggs. Mix well. Transfer to a serving dish. Cover and chill for 1 to 2 hours before serving.

GREEN CHILE SCONES

MAKES 6 SERVINGS

This simple scone is dense, simple, and savory. It is perfect for dipping in a warm stew or just slathered with butter. Green chile and Parmesan cheese blend well in this scone to create a hearty bread.

> 2 cups flour
> 2 tsp. baking powder
> 1 ¼ tsp. salt
> Pinch of black pepper
> ⅓ cup Parmesan cheese, shredded
> 1 stick butter, chilled and cut into 8 pieces
> 1 egg, whipped
> ⅓ cup whipping cream; reserve 1 tbsp.
> 1 cup Hatch green chile, roasted, peeled, seeded, and minced
> Hatch Hot Honey (95) (optional)

1. Preheat oven to 400. Prepare a baking sheet with parchment paper.

2. In a large bowl combine flour, baking soda, salt, and pepper. Add shredded cheese and butter, one piece at a time. Mix well until crumbly.

3. Whisk egg and cream together but do not over stir. Add to the flour mixture, slowly, kneading with your hands, until mixed well.

4. Pat green chile with a paper towel to dry it. Gently fold green chile into the flour mixture until well blended.

5. Pat and shape dough into a round ¾- to 1-inch high on the baking sheet.

6. Brush the top with remaining cream.

7. Using a knife that you've run under cold water, slice the round into 6 wedges, not moving them from the round.

8. Bake for 30 to 40 minutes until lightly browned. Remove from oven and serve immediately with Hatch Hot Honey.

HATCH GREEN CHILE CORN BREAD

MAKES 6 TO 8 SERVINGS

A simple corn bread is comforting with a side of beans, barbequed chicken, or a bowl of chile. Add some green chile, cheese, and corn, and a simple corn bread offers a depth of flavor. This recipe creates a hearty tasty bread.

> 2 sticks butter, chilled and cut into pieces
> 4 eggs
> ½ cup sugar
> 1 cup flour
> 1 cup cornmeal
> 1 tbsp. baking powder
> 1 tsp. baking soda
> ½ tsp. Kosher salt
> 1 cup hot Hatch green chile, roasted, seeded, peeled, and chopped
> 1 cup whole corn kernels
> 1 cup Monterey Jack cheese, shredded
> 1 tbsp. vegetable shortening or lard

1. Preheat oven to 400 degrees.

2. In an electric stand mixer, using a paddle attachment, mix butter and eggs until smooth, about 8 minutes.

3. In a separate bowl, combine sugar, flour, cornmeal, baking powder, soda, and salt.

4. Slowly add flour mixture to egg mixture and mix well on low. Fold in chile, corn, and cheese. Mix well.

5. Place shortening in an 11 × 7 in. baking pan and place in oven to melt, about 3 minutes.

6. Remove baking pan from oven.

7. Reduce heat to 375 degrees. Pour batter into pan and spread evenly.

8. Bake for 20 minutes, then turn pan around and bake another 30 minutes until the top is lightly brown and center is firm and springs back when touched. Remove and serve immediately.

CHILE GARLIC TOAST

MAKES 10 TO 12 SLICES

I love garlic toast, so naturally I would add a bit of Hatch chile to top it off. This scrumptious golden-brown, crispy bread crowned with a cheesy chile mixture can be paired with any entrée, salad, or soup.

> 1 cup butter, softened
> 1 ½ tsp. granulated garlic*
> 1 loaf French bread, cut into 1 ½-inch-thick slices
> 1 cup Hatch green chile, roasted, peeled, seeded, and chopped
> 2 cups Monterey Jack cheese, grated
> 1 tbsp. olive oil

1. Preheat oven to 325 degrees.

2. In a small bowl, combine butter and granulated garlic. Spread a thin layer of butter on one side of each bread slice. Place side-by-side on a baking sheet.

3. In a medium bowl, combine chile, cheese, and olive oil. Blend well.

4. Top each slice evenly with cheese mixture. Bake until bubbly and lightly browned, about 12 to 14 minutes. Serve immediately.

* Granulated garlic adds garlic flavor without additional salt.

GREEN CHILE CHEESE BREAD

The authentic aroma and taste of a yeast bread is so inviting. This round of fresh-baked crusty bread spiked with green chile is a delight. The process is a bit long but worth the wait.

> 1 tsp. instant or rapid-rise yeast
> 3 cups all-purpose flour
> 1 ¾ tsp. kosher salt
> 1 ¼ cup Monterey Jack cheese or cheddar cheese, grated
> 1 cup Hatch green chiles, roasted, peeled, seeded, and chopped
> 1 ½ cups water

1. In a large bowl, combine yeast, flour, and salt. Gently fold in chiles and cheese.

2. Add water and mix until well blended.

3. Cover bowl with plastic wrap and set aside overnight for 12 to 14 hours.

4. Preheat oven to 450 degrees. When ready, place a greased cast-iron pot with a lid in oven and heat the pot for about 30 minutes.

5. While pot is heating up, place dough onto a heavily floured surface and shape into a ball. Cover with plastic wrap for 30 minutes at room temperature.

6. Carefully, remove hot pot from oven and place the dough inside and dust with a little flour. Cover and return to oven and bake for 30 minutes. Uncover and bake an additional 15 minutes until golden brown. Remove bread from oven and carefully place on a baking rack to cool. Slice and serve.

TEXANS LOVE HATCH CHILE!

I try to visit one of the Central Market grocery stores in Texas every August to experience their version of the Hatch Chile Fest. It is a culinary adventure! Spicy food–loving Texans get their Hatch chile fix during this two-week fest at the ten different Central Market stores between Dallas, Waco, Austin, San Antonio, and Houston. This on-site promotional event is truly an occasion that brings the community together.

Chile welcome at Central Market in Dallas.

In the early 2000s T. J. Runyan of Mesilla Valley Produce and Chris Franzoy of Young Guns Chile created a special relationship with the produce buyers of Central Market. I worked with Edward Avalos and James Ditmore in the New Mexico Department of Agriculture as a chile ambassador traveling from store to store on chile promotion and training. It was a true culinary immersion.

Today, tons of chile are shipped in for the event annually. The Central Market team creates delicious chile-infused food items for every food category: from the bakery's Hatch chile brownies and Hatch chile cheese bread to the butcher shop's Hatch chile–stuffed beef rolls, Hatch Chile Marinated Chicken, and Hatch Crab Cakes. Additionally, I counted over fifty prepackaged culinary items throughout the store created with Hatch chile: cookies, crackers, chips, popcorn, spreads, and pickles. Fascinating! The chile-focused cooking classes are loads of fun and include lots of tastings. All while the produce guys roast chile and visit with customers. A fun day at the grocery store . . . literally!

149

Central Market grocery chain of Texas welcomes Hatch chile every August, offering tons of Hatch chile for their chile-loving customers.

5 SOUPS AND STEWS

HATCH IS A GROWING COMMUNITY OF welcoming personalities, set in a beautiful rural environment. Wandering through the small farming village you will see strings of red chile ristras hanging outside local businesses, gracing the doorways, and decorating patios, reminding us that green chile soon turns to red as the winter months envelop the landscape of the valley.

Today, more and more second- and third-generation families proudly call Hatch, New Mexico, home. Farming is strong, tourism is increasing, and the local business community is thriving.

You can always count on the earthy scent of roasting chile lingering in the air in those early fall months, much like the aroma in the kitchen of a warm soup or chowder simmering on the stove. Soups and stews are healthy and hydrating, they are high in fiber, and they help to introduce more veggies into our everyday diets, providing more vitamins and minerals.

This collection of recipes offers a combination of red and green chile flavors in seasoned broths and creamy chowders.

151

I have included simple ingredients and easy techniques so you can create flawless soups, stews, and chowders. Enjoy traditional favorites like Hatch Red Chile Pork Posole and Albondigas Sopa, along with some infused recipes like Hatch-Style Gumbo, a Cajun favorite with a Hatch chile kick. I serve these soups, chowders, and stews in big bowls with plenty of crusty breads. Add a drizzle or splash of my sauces or salsas for additional flavor. My Hatch Chile Salsa Verde, Chile Avocado Salsa, or Hatch Chile Dipping Oil will elevate these bowls of goodness in new and delicious ways. So create, whisk, boil, simmer, and infuse these yummy soups and stews with Hatch chile!

(*opposite page*) Freshly strung Hatch red and green chile ristras drying in the New Mexico sun.

LOBSTER BISQUE LACED WITH RED CHILE

MAKES 6 TO 8 SERVINGS

This homemade bisque will make a meal special. It's a creamy bisque, rich in garlic and cream, flecked with Hatch red chile and succulent lobster meat. A good bowl of bisque with a crusty piece of bread is always a favorite.

2 tbsp. olive oil
2 cloves garlic, minced
¾ cup carrots, diced
2 ribs celery, diced
1 medium onion, finely chopped
2 tbsp. tomato paste
3 tbsp. flour
1 ½ tsp. Hatch red chile powder (Hatch Chile Marketplace, 175), divided
1 ½ cups dry white wine
4 cups lobster or seafood stock
1 cup heavy cream
2 tbsp. butter
12 to 14 oz. lobster meat, cooked, divided*
1 tsp. salt
Ground black pepper to taste
Chives, minced

1. In a large stock pot, sauté garlic, carrots, celery, and onion in olive oil over medium heat. Sauté until vegetables soften, 4 to 6 minutes.

2. Add tomato paste and gently stir to coat vegetables.

3. Sprinkle flour and ½ tsp. red chile powder over vegetables and coat. Cook, stirring quickly so as not to burn, about 1 to 2 minutes.

4. Add wine to deglaze, using a flat spoon or spatula to stir and scrape the bottom of the pan. The mixture will reduce and thicken. Simmer for 8 to 10 minutes.

5. Use an emulsifier in the pot to blend and puree vegetables and wine (or carefully transfer to a blender). Puree until smooth.

6. Combine puree with 3 cups of lobster/seafood stock in pot and simmer for 30 minutes.

7. Add cream, butter, and lobster pieces, reserving about ½ cup lobster for garnish. Add salt and pepper and gently blend well. Add remaining 1 cup of stock for desired thickness. Garnish with chives, lobster, and remaining chile powder.

8. Serve immediately or cool and transfer to an airtight container and refrigerate for 2 to 3 days.

* Boil 4 (3 to 4 oz.) lobster tails until firm. Remove from shell and cut into small pieces. Reserve lobster stock.

HATCH ITALIAN ZUPPA

MAKES 4 TO 6 SERVINGS

This garlicky, brothy wonder is packed full of spices and greens—light but filling. Hatch green chile pairs well with Italian flavors for this hearty soup.

        1 lb. Italian sausage
        1 tsp. red pepper flakes
        3 tbsp. butter
        1 medium onion, diced
        4 garlic cloves, minced
        1 ½ cups Hatch green chile, roasted, peeled, seeded, and chopped
        6 cups chicken broth
        2 cups water
        4 golden potatoes, washed and cut into 1-inch pieces
        3 cups fresh spinach leaves, rinsed
        2 cups heavy cream
        ¾ cup Parmesan cheese, grated

1. In a large pot, sauté sausage and red pepper flakes over medium heat until browned and crumbly. Remove sausage from pot and set aside.

2. In the same pot, add butter and sauté onions until softened, about 3 to 4 minutes. Add garlic and chile and sauté until fragrant, about 1 minute.

3. Stir in chicken broth and water and bring to a boil over high heat.

4. Add potatoes and cook until tender, about 20 minutes.

5. Reduce heat to medium, adding spinach, cream, and cooked sausage. Cook and stir until spinach is wilted and all ingredients are heated through.

6. Garnish with Parmesan cheese and serve immediately or cool and transfer to an airtight container and refrigerate for 2 to 3 days.

HATCH POT O' BEANS

MAKES 6 SERVINGS

I take great comfort in coming home to a dinner as simplistic as this . . .
a bowl of pintos and chile. As a main or side dish, these beans are hearty
and filling. The secret is the balance of flavor: pintos and ham with an
accent of green chile. Fiber-rich and tasty, it's a "go to" for any time of year
but so inviting during those cooler months.

> 3 cups dried pinto beans
> Water
> 1 tbsp. onion powder
> 2 cloves of garlic, minced
> 1 onion sliced into rings
> 1 cup Hatch green chile, roasted, peeled, seeded, and chopped
> 1 ½ cups diced lean cooked ham
> Salt to taste
> ½ cup cilantro leaves
> 1 to 2 avocados, diced
> 1 tsp. Hatch red chile powder (Hatch Chile Marketplace, 175)

1. Drain and sort beans, removing any debris.

2. Place beans in a large stock pot. Add water to cover and soak for 6 to 8
   hours. Drain.

3. In the same pot add water and cover beans by 4 inches.

4. Cook over high heat, bringing to a boil.

5. Reduce heat to medium high and boil gently for 1 hour. Add garlic, onion powder, onions, green chile, and ham.

6. Continue boiling covered until beans are soft, about another 1 ½ to 2
   hours. Add salt to taste. Garnish with cilantro, avocado, and red chile
   powder. Serve immediately in individual bowls. or cool and transfer to
   an airtight container and refrigerate for 2 to 3 days.

BACON AND POTATO GREEN CHILE CHOWDER

MAKES 4 TO 6 SERVINGS

There are so many versions of potato soup . . . cheesy, creamy, and rich, of course! But adding spice with green chile takes the lead. A bowl of comfort with a bit of surprise is what you will find in this recipe. It is filled with tender potatoes floating in a creamy base spiced with chile.

> 6 slices thick bacon
> 2 tbsp. olive oil
> ⅓ cup flour
> 2 garlic cloves, minced
> 1 medium onion, diced
> 1½ cups Hatch green chile, roasted, peeled, seeded, and sliced, divided
> 4 to 5 gold Yukon potatoes, peeled and diced
> 1 tsp. salt
> ½ tsp. black pepper
> 4 cups chicken broth, divided
> 1 cup whole milk
> 1 cup heavy cream
> 1½ cups cheddar cheese, grated
> 4 green onions, minced

1. In a medium-sized skillet, cook bacon over medium heat until crispy, about 6 to 8 minutes. Remove bacon from skillet, leaving bacon drippings. Crumble bacon and set aside.

2. In a small bowl, combine olive oil and flour to create a roux. Blend well. Set aside.

3. In a large stock pot add the bacon drippings, garlic, onion, and 1 cup of the green chile and sauté until softened and onion is translucent, about 4 to 6 minutes.

4. Add potatoes, season with salt and pepper. Cover and cook over

medium-high heat, stirring occasionally, until potatoes are softened, 5 to 7 minutes.

5. Slowly add broth and bring to a boil over high heat. Cook until potatoes are tender but firm, about 10 minutes.

6. In a bowl combine roux and milk, then whisk until smooth. Add milk mixture and cream to the stock pot, stirring as soup thickens. Blend well and simmer over low heat.

7. Serve soup in individual bowls. Garnish each bowl equally with cheese, remaining green chile, bacon, and green onion.

8. Serve immediately.

HATCH GREEN CHILE STEW

MAKES 6 SERVINGS

Green chile stew is such a tradition in our New Mexico cuisine. I always love feeling the fall weather in the air, which calls for a big pot filled with chile, meat, and potatoes. The stew is loaded with meaty chunks and seasoned with Hatch chile and onion. It is perfect as a main meal or a cup on the side.

2 to 3 lbs. top sirloin roast, cut into bite-sized pieces*
7 cups beef stock
3 to 4 cloves garlic, minced
1 ½ tsp. black pepper
2 tsp. ground cumin
1 ½ cups Hatch green chile, roasted, peeled, seeded, and chopped
5 to 6 medium potatoes, washed, peeled, and diced
Salt to taste

1. Place meat in a stock pot. Add water to cover meat by 2 inches. Bring to a boil over medium-high heat and cook until water has evaporated and meat is tender, about 45 minutes to an hour. Watch closely to avoid burning.

2. Add beef stock, garlic, pepper, cumin, and green chile. Bring to a boil over high heat. Add the diced potatoes. Reduce to medium heat and add salt. Cook until potatoes are tender, about 15 to 20 minutes.

3. Simmer for 45 minutes. Add salt to taste. Serve immediately or cool to room temperature and transfer to an airtight container and refrigerate for 2 to 3 days.

Variation: For a Green Chile Pork Stew: omit the sirloin beef and beef stock and substitute 2 to 3 lbs. pork roast, cut into bite-sized pieces, and 3 cups water or vegetable stock and 4 cups water. For a Green Chile Chicken Stew: omit the sirloin beef and beef stock and substitute 3 cups cooked diced chicken and 7 cups chicken stock.
* I also use beef chuck for this recipe.

THE GARAY FAMILY

In 1987 Mary Alice Garay established one of the first female- and minority-owned chile companies in New Mexico. She was joined by her three sons, Frank, Randy, and Patrick, and they started dehydrating, processing, and distributing red chile. Today, this family business has grown into a large producer of a variety of green and red chile products, specializing in dehydrated chile and dry chile products; flame roasted, peeled, and chopped green chile; and homestyle red chile puree. They specialize in large-scale distribution for the food industry and are known for their high-quality chile among culinary professionals. Look for the M. A. and Sons Chile Products at your local market.

HATCH RED CHILE PORK POSOLE (POSOLE ROJO)

MAKES 6 SERVINGS

Posole is a favorite in New Mexico, very popular during the cooler months and holiday season. Regionally, it is often known as a ceremonial dish that celebrates life's blessings. It is a brothy soup filled with a combination of hearty pork, hominy, and spicy red chile.

2 lbs. boneless pork roast, cubed
2 tbsp. salt
3 cloves garlic, minced
1 tbsp. chopped dried Mexican oregano
1 to 2 tsp. ground cumin
1 ½ cups Hatch Red Chile Sauce (112)*
2 to 3 cups canned white hominy, drained and rinsed
2 ½ cups water
1 medium onion, minced
2 limes, quartered

1. Place pork in a large pot. Add just enough water to cover. Bring to a boil over medium-high heat. Reduce heat to medium and boil gently, stirring occasionally, until pork is tender and water and juices have evaporated, watching closely for about 1 ½ hours. Reduce heat to medium low. Stir in salt, garlic, oregano, and cumin, coating all of the meat pieces.

2. Add the sauce and hominy, mixing well. Slowly stir in 2 ½ cups water. Simmer, stirring occasionally, until completely heated through, 10 to 15 minutes.

3. Ladle into individual bowls and garnish with onions and a wedge of lime.

HATCH CHILE CHICKEN POSOLE

MAKES 8 TO 10 SERVINGS

Last holiday season I created this simple posole recipe that calls for rotisserie chicken, saving multiple steps. It is a tasty combination of green chile, chicken, and hominy. You will enjoy the ease in preparation when cooking for a crowd.

> 2 to 3 tbsp. olive oil
> 2 to 3 cloves of garlic, minced
> 2 white onions, minced
> 2 to 3 cups medium/hot Hatch chile, roasted, peeled, and chopped
> 1 rotisserie chicken, skinned and shredded (3 to 4 cups)
> 5 to 7 cups of chicken broth*
> One (108 oz.) can of white hominy, drained and rinsed
> 1 tsp. Mexican oregano
> ¼ tsp. cumin
> Garnish: minced onion, fresh lime wedges, Mexican oregano, sliced radishes, minced cilantro

1. In a skillet, sauté garlic and onion in oil over medium heat until onion is translucent, about 8 to 10 minutes. Add green chile and mix well. Remove from heat.

2. In large stock pot, add the green chile mixture, chicken, and stock. Mix well and cook over medium heat for 10 minutes.

3. Add hominy and bring to a slow boil over medium-high heat. Reduce heat to medium low and add spices. Mix well and cook for 8 to 10 minutes. Taste and add more spice if needed.

4. Serve in individual bowls and garnish generously.

Variation: Hatch Chile Shrimp Posole: Omit chicken and substitute 4 cups cooked, peeled shrimp. Reduce chicken stock by half and add 3 cups water to the stock pot when adding green chile mix and shrimp. Increase cumin to 1/2 tsp. Salt to taste.

* I like to use Knorr chicken bouillon. It is best mixed as 1 tsp. bouillon to 1 cup water. Low-sodium chicken stock is an option as well. For a brothier soup, increase amount of chicken stock.

ALBONDIGAS SOPA

MAKES 4 TO 6 SERVINGS

This soup is a family favorite and a true Mexican tradition in comfort food. It is full of tender little meatballs (*albondigas* means "meatball") floating in a savory tomato broth, laced with Hatch chile and spices.

1 lb. quality ground beef
2 tbsp. long-grain white rice
1 large egg, beaten
¼ cup fresh oregano leaves, minced
1 tsp. salt
½ tsp. Hatch red chile powder (Hatch Chile Marketplace, 175)
1 tsp. freshly ground black pepper
1 tsp. olive oil
1 medium yellow onion, diced
3 cloves garlic, minced
8 cups beef broth
2 tbsp. tomato paste
2 medium carrots, peeled and sliced
6 Hatch green chiles, roasted, peeled, seeded, and sliced or chopped
¼ cup loosely packed cilantro
¼ cup loosely packed flat Italian parsley

1. In a large bowl, combine meat, rice, and egg. Mix in fresh oregano, salt, chile powder, and pepper. Roll into 1-inch balls.

2. In a large pot, heat oil over medium heat. Add onion, stirring until softened, 3 to 5 minutes. Add garlic and cook for 1 minute.

3. Add broth and tomato paste. Increase heat to medium high. Bring to a boil and add carrot slices and cook until carrots are soft, 20 to 30 minutes. Reduce heat to slow boil.

4. Gently add meatballs to boiling broth, one at a time. Add green chile and cover. Cook until meatballs are no longer pink inside and rice is tender, 30 minutes. Reduce heat to low.

5. Ladle into individual bowls. Garnish with cilantro and parsley.

Variation: For a heartier soup add 1 potato, diced into bite-size pieces, when adding the carrots.

HATCH-STYLE GUMBO

MAKES 6 SERVINGS

Cajun flavors with Hatch chile create a complex broth as the backdrop for sausage, chicken, and shrimp. Enjoy the layers of culinary flavor and texture. This gumbo takes some time but is worth the effort.

 ¾ cup all-purpose flour
 ½ cup vegetable oil
 1 lb. andouille sausages, cut into ¼-inch slices*
 6 to 8 cups chicken broth
 3 garlic cloves, minced
 1 ½ cups celery, chopped
 1 yellow onion, diced
 1 cup green onion, diced
 ½ cup Hatch Green chile, roasted peeled, seeded, and chopped
 1 cup fresh flat parsley leaves and stems, chopped
 1 tbsp. Cajun seasoning**
 1 tbsp. Hatch red or green chile powder (Hatch Chile Marketplace, 175)
 2 cups cooked chicken, shredded
 1 cups cooked shrimp, peeled, tails removed and left whole
 3 cups cooked white rice

1. In a large stock pot, combine oil and flour and cook over medium-low heat, stirring constantly. Cook for 8 to 15 minutes until this roux becomes a darker color and doughy in consistency. Watch closely while stirring so as not to burn. Remove from heat.

2. In a large skillet, brown sausage on medium-high heat until crispy, about 3 to 5 minutes. Remove sausage from skillet and set aside, leaving drippings in the pan.

3. Add 1 cup of broth, garlic, onion, and celery to skillet. Deglaze and cook until celery and onion are tender. Pour into stock pot with the roux. Mix well.

4. Pour remaining broth, green chile, and parsley into stock pot. Bring to a boil for 6 to 8 minutes. Add seasonings, sausage, chicken, shrimp, and rice.

5. Reduce heat to medium and cook 10 to 15 minutes. Serve immediately or cool and transfer to an airtight container and refrigerate for 2 to 3 days.

* Andouille is a pork sausage originating from France. Its distinct flavor is a bit smokier and sharper than that of most sausages. Substitute Polska Kielbasa sausage if needed.
** There are quite a few high-quality Cajun spice blends on the market. They are typically a blend of paprika, garlic powder, cayenne pepper, dried oregano, onion powder, salt, and pepper.

GREEN CHILE CHICKEN CHOWDER

MAKES 6 TO 8 SERVINGS

This combination of Hatch green chile, shredded chicken, and kernels of corn folded into a creamy chowder is so delicious. It is local Hatch resident Ellie Hackey's favorite recipe for a quick and easy pot of green chile soup. She says, "The hotter the chile, the better," but any heat level will please the palate. Ellie and her growing family enjoy this chowder year-round.

3 tbsp. butter
2 lbs. skinless cooked chicken, cubed or shredded
3 cups milk
One 23.2-oz. can condensed cream of chicken soup
Two 12-oz. cans whole kernel corn, drained*
1 cup hot Hatch green chile, roasted, peeled, seeded, and chopped**
½ cup favorite tomato-based salsa
¼ cup granulated sugar
2 tbsp. flour
1 tsp. salt
1 tsp. ground pepper

1. In a large Dutch oven pot or heavy stock pot, melt butter over medium heat. Slowly stir in chicken, milk, condensed soup, and corn. Reduce heat to medium low and let simmer until heated through, about 12 to 15 minutes.

2. Slowly add green chile and salsa and mix well. Simmer on low for 5 to 6 minutes.

3. Add sugar, flour, salt, and pepper. Simmer for 4 to 5 minutes until well blended. Serve immediately in individual bowls. Garnish with any of the following: grated cheese, minced green onion, crushed tortilla chips, or cilantro.

* For fresh corn, you can shuck 2 ears of corn, which will yield about 2 cups of corn, then toss into boiling water for 3 minutes and drain. Thawed frozen corn can be used as well.
** Ellie starts with about 8 oz. hot Hatch green chile but adds more to increase the heat level. Adjust flavor to desired taste with an additional pinch of salt and/or sugar.

CREAM OF GREEN CHILE SOUP

MAKES 4 SERVINGS

This smooth and elegant soup combines chile and cream in a savory and delicate way. It is a pureed soup that is smooth and silky. Serve as a first course for an elegant dinner or as the main dish for a light lunch.

> 3 tbsp. butter, divided
> 1 medium onion, chopped
> 2 garlic cloves, minced
> 20 to 25 Hatch green chiles, roasted, peeled, seeded, and minced*
> 2 tbsp. all-purpose flour
> 3 to 4 cups chicken broth**
> 1 cup cream
> Ground black pepper to taste

1. In a large stock pot over medium-high heat, melt butter and sauté onion until soft and translucent, about 3 to 5 minutes. Add garlic and continue to cook until fragrant, about 1 minute.

2. Add chile and sprinkle with flour, stirring until well coated.

3. Slowly add broth, stirring until well blended. Bring to a boil.

4. Remove from heat and cool slightly. Carefully transfer to a blender or food processor, or use an emulsifier in the pot to process, and pulse until very smooth, at least 2 minutes for a velvety texture.

5. Return to pot over low heat. Add cream and pepper. Blend well and cook until heated through.

6. Serve immediately in individual bowls.

* This amount of chile equals 3 to 4 cups of chopped green chile.
** Use 3 cups for a thicker soup or 4 cups for a thinner soup.

CALDILLO

MAKES 6 TO 8 SERVINGS

Colorful vegetables brighten this delicious brothy soup, a Mexican favorite that brings the harvest together. It is a light broth loaded with potatoes, tender sirloin, and green chile. I often garnish each bowl with a scoop of Spanish rice for a bit more texture and flavor.

> 2 lbs. boneless beef top sirloin or round, cut into bite-size cubes
> 3 cloves garlic, minced
> 1 tbsp. onion powder
> 1 tsp. ground cumin
> 3 cups beef broth
> 3 cups chicken broth
> 1 large carrot, cut into medallion slices
> 1 celery stalk, sliced
> 1 zucchini, sliced
> 6 small red potatoes, cut into bite-size pieces
> 1 cup Hatch green chile, roasted, peeled, seeded, and chopped
> 2 cobs corn, cooked and each cut crosswise into 6 pieces
> Salt and freshly ground black pepper
> Hatch red chile powder (Hatch Chile Marketplace, 175) (optional)

1. Place meat in a large stock pot. Add enough water to cover. Bring to a boil over medium-high heat. Cook meat, stirring occasionally, watching closely, until all water and juices have evaporated and meat is tender, about 1 to 2 hours.

2. Add garlic, onion powder, and cumin to the meat and stir until meat is well coated.

3. Add the beef and chicken broths. Bring to a boil over medium heat. Stir in carrots, celery, zucchini, potatoes, and chile. Season with salt and pepper to taste. Boil until the potato is tender, about 15 to 20 minutes.

4. Add corn and cook for 15 minutes more. Divide evenly into individual bowls. Garnish with red chile powder.

CHICKEN TORTILLA SOUP

MAKES 4 TO 6 SERVINGS

Layers of flavor define this soup. This family favorite starts with a basic chicken soup spiked with chile, then topped off with tortilla chips, creamy cheese, a little more chile, fresh avocado chunks, and a bit of cilantro. It is a good choice for a crowd and can be doubled easily.

2 tbsp. olive oil
1 medium white onion, chopped
3 cloves garlic, minced
¾ cup Hatch green chile, roasted, peeled, seeded, and minced
6 cups chicken broth
2 tbsp. tomato paste
2 cups cooked chicken, shredded
2 cups corn tortilla chips or strips, broken
2 cups Monterey Jack cheese, shredded
1 tbsp. Hatch red or green chile powder (Hatch Chile Marketplace 175)
2 avocados, diced
2 tbsp. cilantro, minced
¾ cup sour cream

1. In a large pot, heat oil over medium heat. Add onion, garlic, and chile. Cover and cook, stirring occasionally, until onion is transparent, 4 to 6 minutes.

2. Add broth, tomato paste, and chicken. Reduce heat to low. Cover and simmer for 15 minutes.

3. To serve, divide chips equally in each serving bowl and ladle soup over chips. Top with equal amounts of cheese. Garnish each bowl with a pinch of chile powder, avocado chunks, and cilantro. Top each bowl with a dollop of sour cream.

HATCH CHILE MARKETPLACE

THE WORD IS OUT: HATCH CHILE is awesome! Look for authentic Hatch chile in local markets, culinary centers, restaurants, and grocery stores. As I have said, Hatch chile is known around the world, and availability is getting better every day!

This cookbook is full of recipes that call for fresh Hatch chile, dried chile, ground chile powder, prepared sauces, and spice mixes. I love heading up to Hatch to get these products, but that is not possible for everyone. So here are some great food retailers that will ship Hatch chile products directly to you.

For a more extensive list visit the New Mexico Department of Agriculture website: www.elevatenmag.com.

505 Southwestern Brands
Sauces, Salsas & Handheld Snacks
www.505southwestern.com
Instagram: @505southwestern
Facebook: 505 Southwestern

The Bossy Gourmet
3655 Research Dr.
Las Cruces, NM 88003
(575) 323–0979
www.thebossygourmet.com
Facebook: The Bossy Gourmet
Salsa

Bueno Foods
P.O. Box 293
Albuquerque, NM 87103
(800) 888–7336
www.buenofoods.com
bffeedback@buenofoods.com
Instagram: @buenofoods
Facebook: Bueno Foods

Chile Fanatic
251 West Hall St.
Hatch, NM 87937
https://hatch-chile-peppers.com/

Chopped Chile Company
www.choppedchileco.com
Instagram: @choppedchileco

Farmesilla
1840 Avenida de Mesilla
Las Cruces, NM
(575) 652–4626
www.farmesilla.com
Instagram: @farmesilla
Facebook: Farmesilla

The Fresh Chile Company
320 Wyatt Dr., Suite C
Las Cruces, NM 88001
(575) 800–8284
service@freshchileco.com
www.freshchileco.com
Instagram: @freshchileco
Facebook: Fresh Chile
Facebook Group: Fresh Chile
Cookin!

Hatch Chile Company
www.hatchchileco.com
Instagram: @hatchchileco

Hatch Chile Express
657 Franklin St.
Hatch, NM 87937
(800) 292–4454
www.hatchchileexpress.com

Hatch Chile Market-Grajeda Farms
205 Franklin St.

Grajeda Farms
1007 NM-HWY 26
Hatch, NM 87937
(575) 267–0296
Facebook: Grajeda Hatch Chile
Market

Hatch Chile Store
(575) 635–4680
www.hatch-green-chile.com
support@hatch-green-chile.com
Instagram: @hatchgreenchile
Facebook: The Hatch Chile Store

La Posta Chile Company
P.O. Box 87
Mesilla, NM 88046
(575) 556–9950
www.lapostachileco.com
info@LaPostaChileCo.com
Instagram: @lapostachileco

La Reina Chile Company
www.lareinachile.com
Instagram: @lareinchileco
Facebook: La Reina Chile
Products and La Reina Chile
Company

Ol Gringo Salsa Company
1447 Certified Pl. Building 1-A
Las Cruces, NM 88007
(877) 265–2771
www.olgringosalsacompany.com
Instagram: @olgringochile
Facebook: Ol' Gringo Chile Co.

JEFF WITTE, NEW MEXICO DIRECTOR/SECRETARY OF AGRICULTURE

"We have the best farmers in the world!" says Jeff Witte of the New Mexico Department of Agriculture.

Over the eleven years that Secretary Witte has been in office, the production and promotion of Hatch chile has improved and increased dramatically. "The growers are sophisticated," says Witte, "creating their own products and ways of processing chile."

Hatch chile is a natural, sought-after ingredient for high-end culinary cooking, and with the support of the New Mexico Department of Agriculture we are seeing a sharp increase in the number and variety of national contracts in the processed-foods industry.

"Everybody wants our chile," Witte says. This is why Hatch—and New Mexico—is known as the Chile Capital of the World.

Secretary of Agriculture Jeff Witte enjoying a World-Famous Green Chile Cheeseburger at Sparky's

Paulita's New Mexico
www.paulitasnewmexico.com
Facebook: Paulita's New Mexico

Village Market
418 W. Hall St.
Hatch, NM 87937
(575) 267–4141
Facebook: Village Market

Young Guns Hatch Valley Chile
www.yghatchchile.com
Instagram: @younggunshatch
greenchile
Facebook: Young Guns Hatch
Green Chile

Zia Hatch Chile Company
www.ziahatchchileco.com
Instagram: @ziahatchchileco
Facebook: Zia Hatch Chile
Company

Locally owned eateries in Hatch continue to grow, with new ones popping up all the time. While these restaurants may not ship Hatch chile, you can sit and enjoy fresh chile dishes at your leisure. They enjoy serving chile lovers from around the world.

B&E Burrito
303 N. Franklin St.
Hatch, NM 87937
(575) 267–5191
Facebook: B&E Burritos

Icebox Brewing Company
Hall Street, Hatch, NM 87937
www.iceboxbrewing.com
Instagram: @iceboxbrewing
Facebook: Icebox Brewing Company

Pepper Pot
250 W. Hall St.
Hatch, NM 87937
(575) 267–3822
Facebook: The Pepper Pot
Restaurant

Sparky's Burgers, Barbeque, and
Espresso
115 Franklin St.
Hatch, NM 87937
www.sparkysburgers.com
Instagram: @Sparkysburgers
Facebook: Sparkys BBQ and
Espresso

Valley Café
360 W. Hall St.
Hatch, NM 87937
(575) 267–4798

Village Market Deli
418 W. Hall St.
Hatch, NM 87937
(575) 267–4141
Facebook: Village Market

NEW MEXICO
CHILE
ALL OVER THE NATION

Working with the New Mexico Department of Agriculture (NMDA) in promoting chile is fun and rewarding. Talk about passion! The marketing team at NMDA not only loves Hatch chile they are passionate about promoting Hatch chile worldwide. They work year round but once the chile season begins they will travel across the United States hosting chile roasts at grocery stores, culinary markets, conferences and food shows, sharing the good flavors of Hatch chile.

Much of the success and popularity of Hatch chile goes to the efforts put forth by our team at NMDA. They support and encourage the growers and processors, and engage the consumer every day. Their resources help connect you to your favorite chile products. *So explore and enjoy!*

NEW MEXICO
TASTE THE TRADITION®

NEW MEXICO
GROWN WITH TRADITION®

6 BURGERS, SANDWICHES, AND FLATBREADS

HATCH IS AN ALL-AMERICAN SMALL TOWN, a rural, agricultural community full of hospitality that welcomes visitors to explore, enjoy, and stay awhile. Every time I stop in at the Hatch Chile Express to buy my spices or load up on chile, I visit with Jo Lytle or her daughter Rhonda. We talk food, chile, and what is happening in the community. Same with Teako Nunn, over at Sparky's—he is genuinely interested in people. I enjoy our conversations focused around food and the restaurant industry. It is a community where the residents value individuality, variety, and uniqueness. Art Alba of Village Market enjoys showing customers the store's large local salsa section. He will give background information and flavor recommendations on every salsa they carry, and that is a lot.

Most stores sell "everything" chile. Community recipes and chile cooking techniques are shared from here to there. My visits are always unique and interesting.

I like to think of this collection of recipes as pub food. A burger, a sandwich, or flatbread you can pair with a beer, a glass of wine, or a cocktail. These handheld favorites are full of interesting ingredients and flavor combinations. They are convenient, nostalgic, easy, and comforting, with a variety of flavors. Customize and create your own handheld favorite—or "Grab and Go's," as I call them.

Flatbreads are pizza-like and give us a canvas to create culinary

(*opposite page*) Red chile ristras at Grajeda Farms on Highway 26.

goodness. An easy dough makes this flatbread quicker and easier than pizza. Bites full of homemade free-formed crust brushed with olive oil and topped with spicy meats, fresh herbs, and rich cheeses are addictive.

Additionally, I offer a variety of sandwiches packed full of cured meats and fresh vegetables with layers of flavor, slathered, drizzled, or smeared with my favorite spreads and sauces and nestled in crusty breads, soft buns, or thick slices of artisan breads.

Now let's talk burgers. We know it is an American icon, no doubt, but it is also one of the world's most popular foods. We enjoy western burgers, ranch burgers, bacon burgers, and Hawaiian burgers. Yesssss! We love our burgers. But New Mexico has a burger that has gained fame and popularity over several decades: the green chile cheeseburger. Even more notably, the HATCH Green Chile Cheeseburger. This burger is headlining menus around the world and for good reason! It's a simple, well-seasoned, grilled beef patty topped with fresh Hatch chile and melted cheese and sandwiched between a soft bun. Delicious!

However, you may want infuse even more flavor into your Hatch Green Chile Cheeseburger. Add a little Hatch Bacon Jam, or Hatch Red Chile BBQ Sauce, or maybe Hatch Chimichurri or Whipped Blue Cheese and Chile Cream. You can find all of these in chapter 3: Salsas, Sauces, and Culinary Accents section of this book.

HATCH RED CHILE BURGER

MAKES 4 SERVINGS

Red chile adds a distinct earthy, rich flavor to this cheeseburger. This chile cheeseburger is quirky and delicious. It can be served any time of the day but is perfect for brunch or late-night dining. Add a slice of bacon or top this burger with fries. Customize it to make it your special burger.

> 2 lbs. ground beef*
> 2 tsp. Hatch Red Chile Salt (122)
> 4 Kaiser rolls or hamburger buns
> 1 tbsp. oil
> 4 eggs
> 2 cups Hatch Red Chile Sauce (112), warmed
> 4 slices aged cheddar or American or white American cheese
> 3 green onions, chopped
> ½ cup cilantro leaves
> 1 tsp. Hatch red chile powder (Hatch Chile Marketplace, 175)

1. In a large bowl combine meat and salt. Shape into 4 patties.

2. In a large skillet over medium heat cook patties for 4 to 6 minutes. Flip over and cook another 4 to 6 minutes until medium well or until desired doneness. Remove from skillet and place on bottom bun.

3. Preheat broiler to melt the cheese.

4. In a skillet add oil, then fry eggs over medium heat, over-easy or sunny side up as desired. Keep warm.

5. Top each burger with equal amounts of chile sauce and cheese. Place in broiler to melt cheese, about 2 to 3 minutes. Remove from oven and top each burger with cooked eggs.

6. Garnish with chopped green onion, cilantro, and chile powder. Place top bun and serve.

* I typically use 80/20 split ground beef. Occasionally, I often combine 1 lb. ground beef and 1 lb. ground pork (not ground sausage) for a unique flavor.

HATCH GREEN CHILE CHEESEBURGER

MAKES 4 SERVINGS

This is what New Mexico is famous for! The star of the show . . . A Hatch Green Chile Cheeseburger is always a crowd pleaser. We like them thick and juicy, thin and crispy, grilled, charbroiled, and pan fried. Our local chile lovers have turned an All-American classic into a New Mexico classic by piling it high with fresh roasted Hatch green chile.

> 2 lbs. ground chuck beef*
> 1 tbsp. Worcestershire sauce
> 1 tbsp. Hatch Red Chile Salt (122, or Hatch Chile Marketplace , 175) (optional)
> 2 cups Hatch green chile, roasted, peeled, seeded, and sliced or chopped**
> 4 thin slices aged cheddar, American, or white American cheese
> 4 hamburger buns or soft round rolls
> Mustard (optional)
> 1 onion, sliced into rings (optional)
> 1 large tomato, thinly sliced (optional)
> 1 ½ cups iceberg lettuce, shredded (optional)

1. Preheat grill to medium heat.***

2. In a large bowl combine meat and Worcestershire sauce and shape into 4 patties.

3. Place patties on the grill, sprinkle with chile salt, and cook for 4 to 6 minutes. Flip over and top with equal amounts of chile and a slice of cheese. Cook for another 4 to 6 minutes until medium well or until desired doneness. Cheese should be bubbly and melted. Gently place patties on the bottom buns and cover with top buns smeared with a thin layer of mustard.

4. Serve with onion, tomato, and lettuce on the side.

Variation: For a Double Hatch Green Chile Cheeseburger, start with 3 lbs. of ground chuck divided into 8 patties. Follow the rest of the recipe as directed, using two patties for each hamburger.

* I typically use 80/20 split ground beef. Also, I often combine 1 lb. ground beef and 1 lb. ground pork (not ground sausage) for a unique flavor.

** I like to change up my chile topping by roasting eight whole Hatch Green chiles, then thinly slicing them; or I will use Hatch autumn roasted chile (Hatch green chile that is picked late in the harvest and has started to turn from green to orange, sometime with a bit of red [Hatch Chile Marketplace, 175]), which adds color and flavor.

*** Alternatively, for a stove-top version, place patties in a large skillet and pan fry burgers over medium heat. Follow the recipe as directed.

SWEET HATCH CHILE BURGER

MAKES 4 SERVINGS

I was inspired by a unique combination of West Coast flavors to create this sweet, savory burger. Creamy cheese melting over a sizzling burger crowned with a sweet jelly and caramelized onions is amazing. It is an upscale burger full of Hatch chile flavors.

2 lbs. ground chuck beef*
2 tsp. salt.
1 tbsp. Hatch chile seasoning (Hatch Chile Marketplace, 175)
4 oz. goat cheese
4 hamburger buns or Kaiser rolls
4 tbsp. Hatch Chile and Jalapeño Jelly (93)
2 cups arugula greens
1 small red onion, thinly sliced

1. Preheat grill to medium heat.**

2. In a large bowl combine meat and seasonings, blending well.

3. Shape into 4 patties and place on the grill. Cook for 4 to 6 minutes, then flip over and cook another 4 to 6 minutes until medium well or until desired doneness.

4. Top with equal amounts of cheese, closing grill to allow cheese to melt, about 2 minutes.

5. Gently place patties on the bottom buns. Drizzle with jelly and top with arugula and onion slices. Place top bun on each burger.

* I typically use 80/20 split ground beef. Also, I often combine 1 lb. ground beef and 1 lb. ground pork (not ground sausage) for a unique flavor.
** Alternatively, for a stove-top version, place patties in a large skillet. Pan fry burgers over medium heat. Follow the rest of the recipe as directed.

SPARKY'S BURGERS, BARBEQUE, AND ESPRESSO

They have the best Hatch green chile cheeseburgers around! Teako Nunn and his family have made sure of that, serving nearly one hundred thousand Hatch green chile cheeseburgers annually. This colorful eatery offers fun and comfort, with its unique, nostalgic décor as a backdrop while you indulge in tasty burgers, like the "World Famous," a seven-ounce green chile cheeseburger topped with just enough heat to get your attention.

Sparky's also has the best smokehouse BBQ, brisket sandwiches, chicken entrées, chile-laced shakes and lemonades, and rich, delicious espressos.

Notably, Teako, a James Beard Foundation semifinalist in 2020, will typically be in the kitchen flipping burgers, creating a new espresso with his wife, Josie, or serving customers with his daughter, Michelle. They serve both locals and tourists heading north and south on I-25.

www.sparkysburgers.com

187

Teako flipping World Famous Hatch green chile cheeseburgers at Sparky's.

IMPOSSIBLY GOOD CHILE BURGER

MAKES 4 TO 6 SERVINGS

This burger is a meatless wonder! When we are looking for meat alternatives, flavor is key. I have combined hearty ingredients to create this vegetarian burger. The starchy goodness of the black beans, the fresh mushrooms, and the fragrant spices are the foundation for a satisfying meat replacement.

> 2 cans (14 oz.) black beans, drained and rinsed
> Olive oil
> 3 cloves of garlic, minced
> 1 onion, minced
> 1 cup mushrooms, chopped
> ¾ cup Hatch green chile, roasted
> 1 tsp. cumin
> ½ tsp. granulated garlic
> 1 ½ tsp. Hatch Red chile powder (Hatch Chile Marketplace, 175)
> ½ cup bread crumbs
> 1 egg, whisked
> 1 tbsp. Worchester sauce
> 2 tbsp. mayonnaise
> 1 tsp. salt
> 4 to 6 Kaiser rolls or hamburger buns
> Garnish: fresh greens, sliced onion, and tomato*

1. Preheat oven to 375 degrees.

2. Spread beans on a prepared baking sheet and bake for 10 to 12 minutes until slightly dried out. Cool.

3. In a large skillet over medium heat, sauté olive oil, garlic, onion, mushrooms, and chile until onion is softened, about 5 to 7 minutes. Remove from skillet and place on paper towel to drain excess oil.

4. Place onion mixture in a food processor and add cumin, granulated garlic, chile powder, bread crumbs, egg, Worcester sauce, and mayonnaise. Pulse until smooth, about 2 to 3 minutes.

5. Add beans, then gently pulse but keep chunky, about 2 to 3 minutes. Remove and form patties, about ½ cup per patty.

6. Place patties on a parchment-lined baking sheet. Spray top of each patty with cooking spray. Bake for 12 minutes. Gently turn over each burger and bake for an additional 10 minutes. Remove and place on buns. Garnish with fresh greens, sliced onion, and tomato.

* Garnish with your favorite salsa, sauce, or relish from chapter 3.

HATCH MEATLOAF SANDWICH

MAKES 4 SERVINGS

This hearty, understated sandwich is so popular. The chile-laced glaze baked across the top of each slice brings a zest to this classic filling. It is a comforting, homestyle sandwich full of flavor.

2 tbsp. butter
4 slices sourdough bread
4 slices (½ inch thick) of Hatch Chile Meatloaf (212), warmed
Hatch Red Chile Sauce (112), warmed
2 cups fresh greens
1 jalapeño, thinly sliced
1 red onion, thinly sliced

1. In a large skillet, melt butter and grill a piece of bread on both sides until golden brown and crispy. Repeat with remaining bread.

2. Place grilled bread on individual plates. Top each slice with a slice of meatloaf.

3. Divide sauce evenly over each sandwich. Garnish with greens, jalapeño, and onion slices.

HATCH CHILE PHILLY

MAKES 4 SERVINGS

East Coast meets New Mexico! The Philly Cheesesteak is an East Coast favorite. It's time to raise the bar: ribeye steak and Hatch chile create a better Philly Cheesesteak hoagie sandwich. The thinly sliced ribeye is grilled with sautéed onions and fresh Hatch green chile. The cheesesteak is crowned with melted provolone and stuffed into hoagie rolls. You just can't resist.

4 hoagie rolls
2 tbsp. butter
2 cloves garlic, minced
2 tbsp. oil, divided
1 large onion, sliced
½ tsp. salt
Splash of light beer
1 lb. ribeye steak, thinly sliced*
1 ¼ cup Hatch green chile, roasted, peeled, seeded, and cut in strips
Kosher salt
Freshly ground pepper
8 thin slices provolone cheese
4 tbsp Hatch Chile and Lime Mayo (109)

1. Cut each roll lengthwise ¾ of the way through.

2. In a small bowl, combine butter and garlic. Spread evenly on each roll and grill rolls butter side down in a large skillet or flat griddle over medium-high heat. Remove and set aside.

3. Add 1 tbsp. oil to the skillet and cook onions on medium high, scraping the bottom and sides of the skillet. Add salt, pepper, and a splash of beer to deglaze and cook until caramelized, about 14 to 16 minutes. Remove from the skillet and keep warm.

4. Increase the heat to high and add 1 tbsp. oil to the skillet. Lay meat strips across the skillet, brown for 2 minutes, then turn over and cook another minute or so. Add green chile and cooked onions, moving meat around until all ingredients are heated through.

5. Quickly divide into 4 portions in the skillet and top each portion with 2 slices of cheese. Remove from heat. Cheese will slowly melt, but meat will not overcook.

6. Spread equal amounts of mayonnaise on bottom halves of hoagies. With a spatula, scoop up one portion of meat filling at a time into each hoagie sandwich. Serve immediately.

* Before cutting, wrap raw steak in plastic wrap and place in freezer for 30 to 40 minutes. Remove from freezer and trim excess fat. Using a very sharp knife, cut thin slices against the grain.

CRISPY CHICKEN CHILE SANDWICH

This chicken sandwich is juicy, tender, and well seasoned. My signature chicken sandwich is dripping with red sauce, adding fire and flavor. It's crispy, messy, hearty, and unforgettable.

½ cup panko bread crumbs

2 tbsp. Parmesan cheese

1 egg, beaten

2 boneless, skinless chicken breasts, sliced lengthwise to create 4 thin chicken breast pieces

½ cup oil

¼ cup Louisiana hot sauce

⅓ cup Hatch Red Chile Puree (117)

4 Kaiser buns

¾ cup Monterey Jack cheese, grated

Fresh greens

1. On a plate, mix panko crumbs and Parmesan cheese. In a separate wide, shallow bowl, beat egg.

2. Dip each piece of chicken in the beaten egg and then dip in the panko mixture until well coated.

3. In a large skillet heat oil to 300 degrees over medium-high heat. Add 2 chicken breasts and cook, turning once after 3 to 4 minutes. Cook for another 4 to 6 minutes until golden brown and cooked through (use a meat thermometer to determine when temperature has reached 160 degrees). Remove from skillet. Repeat process with remaining chicken. Place each piece on a plate with a paper towel to catch excess oil.

4. In a medium bowl, combine Louisiana hot sauce and chile puree and warm in microwave or on stovetop. Set aside.

5. Working quickly, dip cooked chicken in the red sauce, allowing excess to drip off. Place each piece on a bottom bun and top with cheese and greens.

THE BACA FAMILY, BUENO FOODS

Ana Baca has fond memories of chile season in New Mexico, sharing, "When we were children, we didn't see our father much between August and October or what we called 'chile season' since he was so busy with the production and processing of fresh green chile. However, once in a while, right before chile season started, we got to accompany him to the chile farms in Hatch as he would visit with the farmers and talk about the forthcoming harvest. We recall following him through the chile fields, getting our shoes muddy, and when we got home, while we bathed and soothed our sunburns, he and our mom roasted a box of chile just picked that morning, peeled it, added fresh garlic, salt, and tomato and served it to us in a Bueno® Tortilla. What a treat! We cannot ever forget that aroma of freshly picked Hatch green chile, roasting in the oven and wafting from the kitchen."

As the vice president of marketing and communications for Bueno® Foods, Ana explains, "Hatch is a geographic designation, just as Napa wines designates where the grapes for the wine are grown. We only use certified Hatch chile in the products that we designate as Hatch. We use the Hatch certification seal on those products. We want Hatch, New Mexico, to thrive." Additionally, "We've processed and sold chile from Hatch and other areas of New Mexico for over seventy years. It is wonderful to see that Hatch chile is nationally and internationally recognized as the best chile in the world."

Ana's family's two favorite chile recipes are calabacitas with Hatch green chile (a traditional medley of corn and squash) and Hatch green chile stew.

Notably, the process of frozen chile goes back to the early 1950s when the Baca Brothers of Albuquerque, New Mexico, realized that every household was getting a home freezer and Birds Eye® foods was rolling out frozen food products. During this time, the brothers had been selling fresh and dried chile but soon developed their idea of roasting fresh chile over an open flame and freezing it. This allowed chile lovers to freeze and store chile so they could enjoy it through the winter until the next August harvest. They created Bueno® Foods, the first to commercially roast and freeze green and red chile. Today the company has multiple products (Hatch Chile Marketplace, 175) and boasts the largest green and red chile freezer in the United States.[1]

Note

1. "Bueno® Foods (2023) Bueno® Timeline," accessed April 18, 2023, https://buenofoods.com/the-bueno-story/.

Four generations of Bacas. Filomena and her father Teofilo Jojola, who farmed in the Hatch area, along with Marcus Baca and Marie Adele Baca. Ana Baca's paternal grandmother's family lived and farmed in the areas around Hatch, New Mexico, in the 1800s. They grew chile and other produce.

HATCH CHICKEN SALAD SANDWICH

MAKES 4 SERVINGS

I love a robust and tasty chicken salad sandwich. This flavor combination—piled high between crusty, grilled sourdough bread; dressed with chile infused oil and a schmear of avocado; and piled high with green chile—is the perfect sandwich.

    8 slices sourdough bread
    4 tbsp. Hatch Chile Dipping Oil (99)
    2 cups Hatch Chile Chicken Salad (128)
    4 whole Hatch green chiles, roasted, peeled, and seeded
    6 leaves butter lettuce
    1 medium red onion, sliced into thin slices
    2 avocados, peeled, seeded, and diced

1. Lightly brush both sides of each slice of bread with dipping oil.

2. In a large skillet, grill each slice over medium-high heat until golden brown, about 2 to 3 minutes on each side. Cool to room temperature.

3. Spread ½ cup chicken salad evenly across 4 slices. Top each with equal amounts of green chile, lettuce, and red onion.

4. Place avocado in a bowl and mash until spreadable. Spread across 4 remaining slices of bread and place avocado-side down on each sandwich.

5. Cut each sandwich in half diagonally and serve immediately.

AVOCADO TORTAS

MAKES 4 SERVINGS

Tortas are a favorite Mexican sandwich. This vegetarian version is packed with veggies, cheese, and fresh avocado. The hummus adds depth of flavor, bringing it all together in a delicious soft roll. I offer a chicken variation that is also delicious.

> 2 tbsp. butter
> 4 soft bolillo rolls, split*
> 2 cups hummus**
> 8 slices Swiss cheese (thinly sliced)
> 2 avocados, peeled and mashed
> 1 cup Hatch green chile, roasted, seeded, peeled, and chopped
> 1 red onion, thinly sliced
> 2 cups fresh greens
> 1 cucumber, thinly sliced
> ½ cup Hatch Chile and Lime Mayo (109)

1. In a large skillet, heat butter over medium heat and lightly toast both sides of each bun.

2. Spread the bottom half of each bun with even amounts of hummus.

3. Top each with 2 slices of Swiss cheese, covering the entire bottom bun. Top cheese slices with equal amounts of avocado, spreading across the entire bun.

4. Top avocado with equal amounts of green chile, onion slices, lettuce/greens, and sliced cucumber.

5. Spread top slices of bread with mayo and place on sandwiches. Slice each sandwich in half and serve immediately.

Variation: For a Chicken Avocado Torta add 2 cups cooked, shredded rotisserie chicken on top of the hummus. Follow the rest of the recipe as directed.

* Bolillo rolls are a crusty Mexican roll, often shaped like a small football. They can be found in most bakery sections at your local market. Soft round rolls also work well. Find your favorite.

** I used a favorite store-bought hummus. Look for a variety of flavors.

HATCH SPICY SUB SANDWICH

MAKES 2 SERVINGS

How about a big Italian sub, Hatch style? It has a combination of cooked and cured meats, Italian spices, spicy oils, and cheese. Green chile only adds to the spicy goodness of this sandwich.

One 12-inch soft loaf Italian bread
¼ cup Hatch Chile and Lime Mayo (109)
4 to 5 oz. Genoa salami, thinly sliced
4 to 5 oz. prosciutto
8 oz. smoked ham, thinly sliced
6 oz. provolone cheese
1 ½ cups chopped iceberg lettuce
2 medium tomatoes, sliced
Salt and pepper
½ cup Hatch Chile Dipping Oil (99)
¼ cup rice vinegar
2 tsp. dried Italian seasoning
Hatch Green Chile Relish (87)
¼ cup kalamata olives, chopped

1. Cut the loaf of bread lengthwise with a serrated knife. Scoop some of the center bread out on the top half of the loaf. Set aside.

2. Spread mayonnaise on the bottom half. Top with salami, prosciutto, ham, and cheese.

3. On the top bun, top the scooped-out side with lettuce and tomato slices. Season with salt and pepper and drizzle generously with dipping oil and vinegar. Sprinkle with Italian seasoning.

4. Top with relish and olives. Carefully bring both halves together. Place on a cutting board, cut in half, and serve immediately.

HATCH PASTRAMI SANDWICH

MAKES 4 SERVINGS

I love a good pastrami sandwich, sometimes just with my Hatch Chile Mustard. But this version has multiple levels of flavor. The pungent horseradish and the creamy chile sauce blend well with the pastrami and cheese to create a one-of-a-kind pastrami masterpiece!

> 2 cups red cabbage, thinly sliced
> ¼ cup Hatch Chile Dipping Oil (99)
> 4 tsp. horseradish
> 8 slices artisan bread or rye, lightly toasted
> 2 lbs. high-quality deli pastrami, thinly sliced, warmed
> 1 cup Hatch Chile Come Back Sauce (106)
> 4 thick slices Swiss cheese

1. Preheat oven to the broil setting.

2. In a small bowl combine cabbage and dipping oil. Mix well and set aside.

3. Spread horseradish on 4 slices of bread. Top each with equal amounts of warm pastrami and place on a baking sheet.

4. Drizzle meat evenly with sauce and top with 1 slice of cheese. Place the remaining pieces of bread on the baking sheet, then place baking sheet in oven and broil until the cheese melts, about 1 to 2 minutes.

5. Remove from oven. Top with equal amounts of cabbage mix. Place other slice of bread on top, slice, and serve.

HATCH CHILE FLATBREAD

MAKES 4 TO 6 SERVINGS

With just a few ingredients you can have fresh, hot flatbread at home. I have played with a few different crust recipes and developed this easy-to-make version. Homemade flatbread is a labor of love.

Crust

- 1 tsp. active dry yeast
- ½ tsp. granulated sugar
- ¾ cup warm water
- 2 cups all-purpose flour
- 3 tbsp. olive oil, divided
- ½ tsp. Hatch red or green chile powder (Hatch Chile Marketplace, 175) (optional)
- 1 tsp. salt

1. In the bowl of a stand mixer with a dough hook, place yeast and sugar. Add very warm water and whisk until blended, then cover and allow to sit for 5 to 7 minutes. Slowly add flour, 1 tbsp. olive oil, chile powder (optional), and salt. Mix on low until blended and stringy, about 3 to 4 minutes.

2. Remove from bowl and knead with hands on a lightly floured surface for 2 to 3 minutes. Place in a greased bowl and cover for 1 hour at room temperature.

3. Punch the dough down and then roll out into a large pizza, or part into 2 pieces of dough and roll out 2 smaller pizzas. Using your fingers, poke each pizza dough and drizzle with 1 tbsp. olive oil.

4. Preheat oven to 400 degrees.

5. Top dough with the toppings suggested below. Bake for 12 minutes, remove, and brush the crust with remaining olive oil. Return to oven for 10 more minutes until the cheese is melted and the edges are golden brown.

Toppings for Flatbread Pizza

Variety is the spice of life, so find your favorite or create your own flatbread! Here are just a few combinations to try.

To make each of these flatbreads, spread olive oil or sauce evenly on one large crust and top with remaining ingredients. Bake as directed above.

HATCH GARDEN FRESH FLATBREAD

4 tbsp. olive oil

4 to 5 cloves garlic, minced

2 tsp. crushed red chile flakes

1 tsp. kosher salt

1 medium tomato, thinly sliced

1 cup Monterey Jack cheese, grated

1 cup mozzarella, grated

½ cup fresh basil

1 cup green chile, roasted, peeled, and chopped

CHILE AND CARAMELIZED ONION FLATBREAD

3 to 4 tbsp. olive oil

1 tsp. kosher salt (optional)

8 to 12 oz. fresh mozzarella, thinly sliced

2 cups Chile-Spiced Caramelized Onions (91)

PESTO SAUSAGE FLATBREAD

2 tbsp. olive oil

1 lb. hot Italian sausage, cooked and crumbled

1 medium onion, minced and cooked

½ cup prepared pesto

2 cups mozzarella, grated

1 ½ cups Hatch green chile, roasted, peeled, seeded, and chopped

GREEN CHILE CHICKEN ENCHILADA FLATBREAD

1 cup Hatch Green Chile Cream Sauce (100)

¾ cup Hatch green chile, roasted, peeled, seeded, and chopped

1 cup cheddar cheese, grated

3 green onions, minced

1 cup cooked chicken, shredded

HOT HONEY AND LEMON FLATBREAD

4 tbsp. olive oil

4 to 5 cloves garlic, minced

½ cup fresh mozzarella, sliced

½ cup fresh basil

¼ cup Hatch Hot Honey (95)

1 medium lemon, thinly sliced

7 ENTRÉES

HOT DAYS AND COLD NIGHTS COMBINE with the altitude, water, climate, and soil of the Hatch Valley to create the perfect growing scenario for the best chile in the world. But it is the people in the valley who bring fresh chile to our tables. Everyone in the area supports the agricultural industry, taking great pride in this crop and the community. You see it wherever you go: chile ristras hanging at the entrances of local businesses or off the neighbors' back porches. Tailgates at high school games are a buffet of chile dishes, and pots of chile are always bubbling behind the trucks at the edge of the football field. Pride is the centerpiece of Hatch and is central to the culture of New Mexico.

The question, "What's for dinner tonight?" speaks to us every night of the week. Here are some recipe ideas for dinner—some tasty pastas, vegetarian recipes, indulgent guest-worthy entrées, and a few savory proteins—all with chile, of course!

Hatch Chile Meatloaf will take you back to your childhood with a new twist of flavor, whereas the aromatic Roasted Chicken with Lemon Chile Glaze elevates this entrée. Hatch Chile Fried Rice and Red Chile Salmon offer tasty and interesting ways to incorporate chile into your culinary world. Tantalizing sauces and seasonings laced with Hatch red and green chile elevate every entrée in this collection. So, explore and create.

(opposite page) Late August Hatch chile harvest at Morrow Farms in the Uves Valley.

CHILE FILET MIGNON

MAKES 2 SERVINGS

Toward late August, at the end of the Hatch chile harvest season, the fresh green chile turns to orange and then to red on the plant. Fresh red chile is fruity and plump and has a hint of sweetness and heat but has to be picked quickly. I like a combination of both fresh red and fresh green combined in a relish to crown this filet mignon. A hint of rosemary accents the bacon and premium meat in a rich and flavorful way.

> Two 4-oz. filet mignon (beef tenderloin)
> 2 thin slices bacon
> 1 tbsp. olive oil
> 1 tsp. Hatch Rosemary Salt (121) divided
> 1 cup Hatch Green Chile Relish (87)
> ¼ cup Hatch fresh red chile, roasted, peeled, seeded, and chopped*

1. Preheat grill to a medium-high heat.

2. Wrap each filet with a piece of bacon and secure with a toothpick that has been soaked in water for 20 minutes.

3. Brush each wrapped filet evenly with oil. Season the top of each with salt.

4. Cook on grill, turning gently until desired doneness, measuring internal temperature with a meat thermometer (135 degrees for medium rare).

5. Plate each filet and garnish with equal amounts of relish and fresh red chile. Serve immediately.

* I have gotten fresh chile in late August/early September in Hatch and around New Mexico. You can also use a processed red chile or a red and green chile mix from the various companies that I have included in the Hatch Chile Marketplace (175).

CHILE-RUBBED RIBEYE

MAKES 2 SERVINGS

This grilled ribeye steak with a lightly crusted chile rub will soon be a favorite. Preseasoning a good cut of meat ensures that it will be flavorful. This steak pairs well with traditional roasted vegetables and buttery potatoes or can be sliced thin and served with Mexican-style frijoles and rice. Either way you can create an amazing meal.

> Two 9-to-12-oz. ribeye steaks
> Hatch Red Chile Rub (123)
> Hatch Red Chile Sauce (112), warmed
> 2 tbsp. olive oil
> 2 tbsp. butter
> ½ cup Monterey Jack cheese, grated
> Simply Pickled Onions (90)

1. In a small saucepan over low heat, melt butter and olive oil until well blended. Brush mixture on each steak generously.

2. Season each steak with chile rub and let stand at room temperature for 30 minutes.

3. Preheat grill to a medium-high heat.

4. Cook on grill, turning gently until desired doneness, measuring internal temperature with a meat thermometer (135 degrees for medium rare).

5. Plate each steak and top with ½ cup sauce. Top with equal amounts cheese and garnish with onions on the side.

DUANE GILLIS'S STEAK AND CHILE MEDALLIONS

MAKES 4 TO 6 SERVINGS

Duane, a fourth-generation chile grower, has eaten Hatch chile just about every way possible. This meaty entrée is a Gillis family favorite. These flavorful roll-ups, seared to a medium rare, are stuffed with Hatch chile, onions, and cheese. Flank steak works well in the recipe due to its lean nature.

> 1 lb. flank steak
> Salt and pepper
> 2 tbsp. olive oil
> 1 clove garlic, minced
> 2 large onions, thinly sliced
> 1 lb. asadero cheese, grated
> 1 cup Hatch green chile, roasted, peeled, seeded, and chopped
> Twine used for cooking
> 1 tbsp. oil

1. Preheat oven to 200 degrees.

2. Lay meat out on a large cutting board and cover with plastic wrap. Flatten with a rolling pin or meat mallet until ¼ inch thick. Remove plastic wrap.

3. Salt and pepper the meat, then let it rest for about 20 minutes.

4. In a medium-sized skillet over medium heat, sauté garlic and onion in olive oil. Cook until the onion is transparent, about 6 to 8 minutes. Stir in chile and cook until heated through, then cool slightly.

5. Spread onion mixture over meat, leaving a 1-inch border around the edges. Top with grated cheese.

6. Roll the meat up by starting at the end closest to you. Roll tightly and slowly all the way across. Secure the roll of meat with cooking twine ties placed across the roll every few inches.

7. With a sharp knife, slice between the twine ties, creating 5 to 7 sliced meat rounds.

8. In a large skillet over medium-high heat, heat oil and sear the meat rounds for 3 minutes on each side, then place in a warm oven to finish for 5 to 10 minutes. Serve immediately.

HATCH CHILE MEATLOAF

MAKES 6 TO 8 SERVINGS

Comfort food never fails. Meatloaf is the perfect "go-to" for weeknight dinners. Adding a bit of red and green chile brings a new addition of flavor and makes this meaty homemade dish memorable.

    1 ½ lbs. ground beef*
    1 egg, beaten
    1 medium onion, chopped
    ½ cup Hatch green chile, roasted, peeled, seeded, and minced
    ¾ cup whole or 2 percent milk
    ¾ cup fine bread crumbs
    1 tsp. salt
    1 tsp. pepper
    ¾ cup Hatch Red Chile BBQ Sauce (98)

1. Preheat oven to 350 degrees.

2. In a large bowl, combine meat, egg, and onion. Mix well.

3. Add chile, milk, bread crumbs, salt, and pepper. Mix until all ingredients are well distributed.

4. Place in a 5 × 9 in. loaf pan and spread evenly.

5. Spread BBQ sauce across the top of the meat liberally and evenly. Bake for 60 minutes. Tent a piece of foil over the top of the meatloaf. Bake for 30 minutes and remove the foil. Return to oven and bake for 30 more minutes. Remove from oven. Let stand for 7 to 10 minutes. Carefully slice and serve.

* I typically use 80/20 split ground beef for flavor.

HATCH CHILE SKILLET CHICKEN

MAKES 4 SERVINGS

Easy skillet comfort food is great for those weeknight dinners. This seasoned chicken is moist, juicy, and easy to make. It sits on a layer of green chile sauce, which adds an element of surprise to each bite.

1 lb. small golden new potatoes
2 tsp. Hatch Rosemary Salt (121)
1 tsp. ground pepper
2 tbsp. vegetable oil
1 ½ lbs. bone-in chicken thighs
2 cloves garlic, minced
5 to 6 sprigs fresh thyme, chopped and divided
Hatch Green Chile Sauce (114)
¼ cup fresh Italian parsley, torn

1. Place potatoes in a microwave-safe dish with about ½ inch of water. Cover and microwave on medium until soft.

2. Salt and pepper chicken pieces. In a large skillet heat oil over medium heat. Add garlic, 3 sprigs of thyme, and chicken, skin-side down, for about 5 minutes, then turn once and cook, covered, for another 5 to 6 minutes, until chicken is cooked through. Remove chicken from skillet and keep warm.

3. In the same skillet, add sauce and heat over medium-low heat.

4. Add chicken and potatoes, gently spooning sauce over both. Cover and simmer for 5 to 8 minutes.

5. Garnish with remaining thyme and parsley. Serve immediately.

GREEN CHILE CHICKEN ALFREDO

MAKES 4 SERVINGS

I have been making this dish for many years. It is a personal indulgence for me. The creamy rich sauce spiked with fresh green chile and crowned with warm, sizzling grilled chicken is a winning combination. Pair it with a favorite wine and enjoy!

> 2 medium chicken breasts
> 1 tsp. salt
> 1 tsp. ground pepper
> One 16-oz. box of linguini or fettucine pasta
> ½ cup Hatch green chile, roasted, peeled, and seeded
> 2 cloves garlic, minced
> 1 tbsp. olive oil
> 1 ½ cups Easy Cream Sauce from the Green Chile Lasagna recipe (216)
> ¼ cup fresh Parmesan cheese, grated
> Fresh oregano

1. Preheat grill to medium heat level.

2. Season chicken breasts generously with salt and pepper. Grill chicken filets over medium heat until juices run clear, about 4 to 6 minutes per side. Transfer to a cutting board and slice into thin pieces. Keep warm.

3. Cook pasta as directed, al dente. Drain of most of the water. Cover and keep warm.

4. In a large skillet, heat oil over medium heat. Sauté chile, garlic, and oil until fragrant, about 1 to 2 minutes.

5. Reduce heat and add sauce, stirring until well blended and heated through. Cover and simmer on very low heat, stirring occasionally for 3 to 4 minutes.

6. Drain pasta and place in a large serving bowl. Toss with warm sauce and top with grilled chicken and Parmesan cheese. Garnish with oregano. Serve immediately.

GREEN CHILE LASAGNA

MAKES 4 TO 6 SERVINGS

Italian flavors infused with green chile create a memorable dish. Our local chefs use chile in so many amazing dishes. This is my version of a local favorite. Green chile is tucked into layers of cheese, creamy sauce, and Italian sausage.

Easy Cream Sauce

> ¼ cup butter
> 1 ½ cups heavy cream
> 2 cloves garlic, minced
> 2 cups Parmesan cheese, freshly grated

1. In a medium skillet, melt butter over medium heat. Add cream and blend well.

2. Slowly blend in garlic and cheese until smooth. Remove from heat.

Lasagna

> One 1-lb. box lasagna pasta noodles
> 2 tbsp. olive oil
> 1 onion, minced
> 2 cups green chile, roasted, peeled, seeded, and chopped
> 1 lb. Italian sausage
> One 15-oz. container fresh ricotta cheese
> 4 ½ cups mozzarella, shredded, divided
> 1 egg, beaten
> 1 tbsp. crushed red pepper flakes

1. Preheat oven to 375 degrees. Spray a 9 × 13 in. baking pan with cooking spray.

2. Cook pasta as directed.

3. In a large bowl combine ricotta cheese, egg, and 1 cup mozzarella. Mix well and set aside.

4. In a large skillet, heat oil with onion and chile until onions are transparent, about 3 to 5 minutes.

5. Add sausage to onion mixture and sauté until browned and cooked through. Set aside.

6. To build lasagna, spread ⅓ cup sauce on bottom of the baking pan. Place a layer of lasagna noodles lengthwise in the bottom of the pan.

7. Top with a layer of sausage mixture, ⅓ of the ricotta cheese, and 1 cup mozzarella cheese. Repeat this process two more times.

8. To finish, top evenly with sauce and remaining 1/2 cup cheese. Cover loosely with foil and bake for 25 to 30 minutes until heated through and bubbly. Garnish with crushed red pepper flakes and serve immediately.

ROASTED CHICKEN WITH LEMON CHILE GLAZE

We always welcome uncomplicated dinners. My honeyed lemon-glazed chicken is easy and elegant. Just a hint of chile adds a distinctive layer of flavor.

> One 2-to-4 lb. chicken
> 2 tbsp. olive oil
> 1 tsp. salt
> ½ cup honey
> Juice of 2 lemons
> 1 tbsp. hot Hatch green chile powder (Hatch Chile Marketplace, 175)
> 1 tbsp. Italian parsley, minced

1. Rinse and pat chicken dry, removing giblets.

2. Place in a prepared baking pan, breast side up, tucking wings under chicken.

3. Brush with oil and season with salt.

4. In a small bowl, combine honey, lemon juice, chile powder, and parsley. Mix well.

5. Bake chicken on lower rack of oven for 45 minutes at 350 degrees.

6. Remove from oven and baste with honey glaze. Continue to cook until the internal temperature reaches 170 to 175 degrees, basting from time to time with honey mixture, about 40 more minutes. Cover with foil if chicken browns too quickly.

7. Remove from oven and brush with remaining glaze. Let stand for 10 minutes before carving.

SEAFOOD-STUFFED HATCH CHILE

MAKES 4 SERVINGS

Fresh seafood salad is delicious, especially served in a fresh Hatch green chile. I love this sweet succulent crab wrapped in a creamy sauce and dusted with chile.

> 1 lb. lump crab meat*
> ½ cup Hatch Chile and Lime Mayo (109)
> ½ cup Hatch green chile, roasted, peeled, seeded, and minced
> ¼ cup white onion, minced
> 1 yellow pepper, seeded and diced
> 4 fresh Hatch green chiles, not roasted
> 1 tsp. Hatch red chile powder (Hatch Chile Marketplace, 175)

1. In a large bowl, combine crab meat, mayonnaise, chile, onion, and yellow pepper. Gently blend well and chill.

2. Split fresh green chiles by slicing them down the center and take the seeds out.

3. When ready to serve, spoon crab filling into each fresh chile. Place on individual plates and dust with red chile powder. Serve immediately.

* I use lump crab that is fully cooked. Check your local market or online.

RED CHILE SAUSAGE ZITI

MAKES 6 SERVINGS

I love everything Italian, so I am always looking for new flavor combinations that highlight this cuisine. Infusing a favorite marinara sauce with Hatch red chile creates a savory, yet spicy sauce. Ziti pasta allows the chile flavor to linger with every bite. Simply Italian is now Simply Hatch Italian!

> 4 cups ziti pasta
> 1 tbsp. olive oil
> 2 cloves of garlic, minced
> 1 lb. Italian sausage
> 1 cup Hatch Red Chile Puree (117)
> 2 cups prepared spaghetti sauce
> 1 ½ cups mozzarella cheese, grated

1. Preheat oven to 350 degrees.

2. Cook ziti as directed on the package; drain most of the water and keep warm.

3. In a large skillet, add oil and garlic and cook over medium-low heat until garlic is fragrant, about 1 to 2 minutes. Add sausage and cook until browned and cooked through. Drain.

4. Add red chile puree and spaghetti sauce to the sausage mixture, cooking and stirring until well blended.

5. In a large bowl, combine ziti and sausage mixture until well blended.

6. Casserole style: Pour into a prepared 9 × 13 in. baking dish. Top with mozzarella cheese.

   Individual style: Divide evenly among ovenproof bowls. Top with cheese and bake for 4 to 5 minutes. Serve immediately.

LEMON CHILE SHRIMP LINGUINI

MAKES 6 TO 8 SERVINGS

This dish is special: rich buttery garlic and lemon sauce with a hint of chile shrimp folded into pasta. I like to fix this in 3 steps because I want the full flavor of garlic, chile, and shrimp shining through.

> 2 medium-sized lemons
> 1 lb. linguini pasta
> 1 lb. or 20 medium shrimp, peeled with tails on
> 1 tbsp. prepared creole seasoning
> 1 tsp. Hatch red chile powder (Hatch Chile Marketplace,175)
> 3 tbsp. butter
> 1 tbsp. olive oil
> 3 garlic cloves, chopped
> 2 tsp. Parmesan cheese, freshly grated
> Pinch of salt and pepper
> ½ tbsp. minced cilantro or Italian parsley

1. Zest and juice one lemon and set zest and juice aside. Discard remaining peel.

2. Cut second lemon into thin slices. Set aside.

3. In a large stock pot bring lightly salted water to a rolling boil. Add linguini pasta, stirring around. Cook for 8 to 12 minutes until al dente; drain almost all water. Keep warm.

4. In a medium bowl, combine shrimp, spices, and the juice of one lemon. Gently toss until well coated. Set aside.

5. In a large skillet over medium heat, melt butter. Add olive oil and garlic, sauté until soft, 1 to 2 minutes. Increase heat to medium high and add shrimp to large skillet; cook until shrimp turns pink, 3 to 4 minutes. Do not overcook. Remove from heat.

6. In stock pot combine linguini pasta and sautéed shrimp, mixing well. Fold in cheese, cilantro or parsley, salt, and pepper to taste.

7. Divide evenly among individual plates. Garnish with remaining lemon slices.

RED CHILE SALMON

MAKES 4 SERVINGS

My son-in-law, who grew up in chile country and loves red chile, created this simple salmon entrée that has become a family favorite. This lightly crusted seasoning adds so much flavor, and the hint of red chile powder enhances the blend of flavors to create a lovely entrée.

> Four 6-oz. salmon filets, skin removed
> 2 tbsp. olive oil
> Hatch Red Chile Salt (122)
> 1 tsp. ground pepper
> 2 lemons, cut in wedges

1. Brush each filet with oil and sprinkle equally with chile salt and pepper.

2. In a large skillet over medium-high heat, cook filets for 5 minutes. Allow fish to sear untouched. Gently turn once, reduce heat, and cook an additional 5 minutes. Using a meat thermometer, check thickest part of the salmon; temperature should be 130 degrees.

3. Remove from skillet, plate, garnish with lemon, and serve immediately.

THE GILLIS FAMILY

The Gillis family arrived in Southern New Mexico in 1918. In 1954 Mary and Dencil Gillis began farming chile and onions while raising their young family in the Hatch Valley. Over time, their enterprise became a family farming operation, with the younger generations working alongside their parents and grandparents.

Speaking about his grandparents, Duane, a fourth-generation farmer, noted, "They worked hard—and lived a long life—and were out on the farm every day. Heck, my grandmother bought a tractor when she was ninety-five! She farmed until she was ninety-eight years old."

Duane and his wife continue the family legacy and work alongside their kids, growing and processing chile, growing onions, alfalfa, corn, and wheat. Duane notes, "We are working to turn it over to the next generation."

Duane loves the climate of the Hatch Valley. "The days are warm and the nights are cool. There are four seasons and mild winters." And he shares the family's love for chile and its health benefits: "We eat chile every day, three times a day; that is why we are all so healthy."

GREEN CHILE SALMON

Elegant and easy! Salmon cooked to perfection is simple enough. But smothered in a spicy wine sauce it truly makes an impression. Great choice for guests and special occasions.

One 2 ½-lb. salmon filet, left whole
2 tbsp. olive oil
2 cloves garlic, minced
1 ½ cups Green Chile Wine Sauce (115), warmed
2 lemons, sliced
½ cup fresh Italian parsley

1. Preheat oven to 325 degrees.

2. Place salmon filet, skin-side down, on a parchment lined, rimmed baking sheet or in a 9 × 13 in. baking dish.

3. Drizzle with olive oil and rub garlic on top.

4. Bake for 18 to 25 minutes. Using a meat thermometer, check thickest part of the salmon; temperature should be 130 degrees. Check thickest part of the salmon for flakiness with a fork.

5. Gently move to a serving platter (move with parchment paper). Drizzle with chile wine sauce and garnish with lemon slices and parsley. Serve immediately.

HATCH HALIBUT

MAKES 4 SERVINGS

Simple but elegant. Your guests will love this light but tasty entrée. This is a light, delicate fish topped with a rich citrusy sauce. Easy oven baking makes this flavorful fish a favorite for the cook.

> Four 6-oz. fresh halibut filets
> ½ cup Hatch Chile and Lime Mayo (109)
> ¼ cup dried bread crumbs
> 1 lemon, cut in wedges
> ¼ cup fresh herbs: Italian parsley, basil, thyme

1. Preheat oven to 425 degrees.

2. Rinse filets and pat dry. Arrange on a parchment paper–lined baking dish.

3. Place halibut in oven and bake until opaque, about 8 to 10 minutes. Fish should flake away easily. Remove from oven and drain off excess liquid.

4. Turn oven to broil. Spread sauce evenly on top of each piece of fish. Sprinkle each filet with bread crumbs and broil for 2 minutes until the top is lightly browned and bubbly.

5. Remove from oven. Plate and garnish each with a lemon wedge and herbs.

THE LYTLE FAMILY

"We are farmers at the core of our being!" says Jo. She and her husband, Jimmy, share a passion for growing in the Hatch Valley. Jimmy is a third-generation farmer, the son of Jim Lytle, who collaborated on the Big Jim Chile variety of Hatch chile. Their family is part of a long line of Hatch chile pioneers. Jim's mother, June Rutherford, is the daughter of Joe Franzoy, one of the first farmers to commercialize Hatch chile. June is revered as the matriarch of Hatch chile, still enjoying and promoting chile today.

Today the Lytles grow several varieties: New Mexico 6-4, Big Jim, and Sandia. They also grow the Lumbre (fire) variety, which was developed and released by Jimmy and Faron, a fourth-generation grower, in 2011.

Jo loves to sell chile and meet people. The Lytles' store, Hatch Chile Express, sits right off I-25. It is where she and her daughter, Rhonda, roast and sell Hatch chile and chile products: fresh (in season), dried, frozen, powdered, seasoning mixes, certified seed, pods, salsas, sauces, and so much more. Jo welcomes her guests with laughter and a love for Hatch and chile.

Their family store has been featured on many cooking and travel shows through the years. Next time you are in Hatch stop by and say hello! For more information see the Hatch Chile Marketplace (175).

HATCH RED CHILE ROASTED PORK SHOULDER

MAKES 4 TO 6 SERVINGS

This rich and delicious pork roast is so easy to prepare. Rub and roast; it's that simple. It is an all-day affair, with the aroma of garlic and chile filling the house. I serve this pull-apart pork with a variety of sauces, like my Hatch Red Chile BBQ Sauce (98), and warm yeast rolls for casual crowd entertaining.

> 2 tbsp. Hatch Red Chile Salt (122)
> ¼ cup granulated sugar
> 2 tbsp. granulated garlic
> One 3-to-4-lb. boneless pork shoulder
> ¼ cup brown sugar

1. In a small bowl, combine chile salt, granulated sugar, and granulated garlic. Mix well.

2. Rinse pork roast and pat dry with paper towels. Rub entire roast with salt mixture. Place in an ovenproof baking dish, cover with plastic wrap or foil, and refrigerate overnight.

3. Remove roast from the refrigerator. Let stand at room temperature for 30 minutes while preheating oven to 300 degrees.

4. Place pork in oven on lower rack. Roast for 3 to 4 hours, basting the roast with its juices every 45 minutes. Using a meat thermometer, check that internal temperature reaches 145 degrees for fully cooked roast throughout. Remove from oven and baste and rub with brown sugar on top and sides.

5. Increase oven heat to 475 degrees, return roast to oven, and cook for 12 minutes until sugar is melted, creating a crusty texture.

6. Remove and let roast set for 8 to 10 minutes before carefully shredding with 2 forks.

7. Serve on a platter with a variety of sauces like Hatch Bacon Jam (96) or Hatch Red Chile BBQ Sauce (98).

HATCH CHILE SPAM MEDLEY

MAKES 2 TO 4 SERVINGS

This is a quirky recipe but a favorite around the Hatch area. Hatch chile sautéed with processed pork became popular after World War II. Hatch local Rena Carson has farmed Hatch chile most of her life with her husband, Nick. Her family enjoys the Spam and chile medley she cooks up every Christmas! Try my version wrapped in a fresh flour tortilla as a side or main dish.

> One 7-oz. can of Spam, chopped*
> 1 tbsp. oil
> 1 onion, chopped
> 1 clove garlic, minced
> 3 ripe tomatoes, chopped
> 8 to 12 Hatch green chiles, roasted, peeled, seeded, and chopped
> Ground pepper to taste
> Seasoning salt to taste

1. In a large skillet, cook the Spam over medium-high heat, stirring and breaking it up, searing some pieces for variety, 10 to 14 minutes. Remove from skillet and keep warm.

2. In the same skillet, add oil, onion, and garlic, and cook over medium-high heat until onion is soft, about 3 to 5 minutes. Add chopped tomatoes and chile, continuing to cook until soft.

3. Reduce heat and add meat back into skillet, season, and simmer for 15 minutes until all ingredients are cooked through. Remove from skillet and serve.

Variation: For Savory, Spicy Spam: Omit onion. Add 2 jalapeños, seeded, cored, and chopped; and 3 green onions, chopped. Cook Spam at medium-high heat until each piece is slightly charred and follow the rest of the recipe instructions.

* This meat is a combination of pork and ham, a little potato starch, and sugar. Created by Hormel in 1937, it has been popular in the Hatch Valley for years.

CHEESY WHITE BEAN RED CHILE BAKE

MAKES 4 TO 6 SERVINGS

I love this upscale bean bake! It is perfect for a fall day, with hearty beans drenched in red chile. Just serve with warm crusty bread and a salad.

> 4 tbsp. olive oil, divided
> 3 to 5 cloves garlic
> 4 tbsp. Hatch Red Chile Puree (117)
> 2 cans (15-oz.) white beans, drained*
> ½ cup boiling water
> ½ tsp. kosher salt
> ⅛ tsp. ground pepper
> 1 ½ cup mozzarella cheese, grated

1. Preheat oven to 425 degrees.

2. In a 10-inch ovenproof skillet or dish, heat 3 tbsp. oil over medium heat and sauté garlic until soft, about 1 to 2 minutes.

3. Stir in red chile puree. Stir until well blended, reducing heat immediately to low.

4. Add beans, water, and salt and pepper. Gently stir to combine.

5. In a small bowl, toss cheese with remaining olive oil. Sprinkle cheese evenly over the top of the beans.

6. Bake for 8 to 12 minutes until cheese is melted and bubbly.

* You can use dried white beans. Soak 3 ½ cups of beans in a large pot of water overnight. Drain and cover beans in stock pot with fresh water. Cook over medium-high heat, covered, until beans are softened, about 1 to 2 hours.

HATCH CHILE FRIED RICE

MAKES 4 SERVINGS

Asian flavors are captivating, and even though they have their own spicy accents, Hatch chile adds even more. Filling and versatile, this dish can go in many directions. You can serve it as is, with an added protein, or as a side dish.

4 cups water
2 cups white rice
2 tbsp. oil
⅔ cup minced carrots, cooked
½ medium red bell pepper, minced
1 cup Hatch green chile, roasted, peeled, seeded, and chopped
2 eggs, beaten
2 to 3 tbsp. soy sauce
1 to 2 tbsp. sesame oil
Hatch Asian Sauce (101)

1. In a large pot over medium-high heat, boil water and add rice. Bring to a boil, reduce heat, and simmer, covered, for 20 minutes until rice is soft and water is absorbed. Set aside.

2. In a large skillet or wok heat oil over high heat. Add carrots, bell pepper, and chile. Quickly cook and stir until tender. Push vegetables to the side and add eggs; whisk until eggs are cooked through. Slowly incorporate vegetables with eggs and add rice, soy sauce, and sesame oil, stirring and cooking until well blended. Reduce heat and mix well.

3. Remove from heat and plate to serve.

Variations: For a heartier fried rice, add 2 cups of cooked and diced chicken, shrimp, or sirloin.

CHILE RELLENO BLACK BEAN BAKE

MAKES 4 TO 6 SERVINGS

Rich in vegetable flavors, this farm-to-table bean bake is complex and delicious. It is a medley of fresh tomato flavors teamed with green chile and topped with a nutty, buttery cheese. The added black beans create a hearty entrée everyone will enjoy.

2 cups Hatch Harvest Salsa (80)
6 Hatch Chile Rellenos (258)
2 cups cooked black beans, drained
1 cup muenster cheese, grated
3 green onions
½ cup cotija cheese, crumbled
1 tbsp. cilantro

1. Preheat oven to 325 degrees.

2. In a large cast-iron skillet, heat salsa over medium heat and sauté until heated through.

3. Gently arrange prepared chile rellenos on top of warmed salsa in the skillet with chile ends toward the middle of the skillet.

4. Spoon beans evenly over each chile relleno, allowing beans to fall into salsa.

5. Sprinkle with muenster cheese. Place in oven for 12 to 15 minutes until heated through and salsa is bubbly.

6. Remove from oven and garnish with onions, cotija cheese, and cilantro. Serve immediately.

SEARED HATCH CAULI STEAKS

MAKES 4 SERVINGS

Thick cuts of cauliflower are deliciously seasoned and roasted to perfection. They can work as a side dish or even a main dish. Seasoned and sauced fresh cauliflower is so versatile and so good with Hatch chile flavors.

> 1 tsp. salt
> 1 tsp. granulated garlic
> 1 tsp. Hatch red chile powder (Hatch Chile Marketplace, 175)
> 1 large cauliflower, cored and sliced into ½-inch slices (4 to 6 slices)
> 2 tbsp. vegetable oil
> ½ cup Hatch Asian Sauce (101) or Hatch Chimichurri (103)

1. Preheat oven to 375 degrees.

2. In a small bowl combine salt, garlic, and chile powder.

3. Brush each cauliflower steak with oil on both sides. Season with salt mixture.

4. Heat a heavy skillet over medium-high heat. Sear each cauliflower steak 2 to 3 minutes on each side. Place on a baking dish.

5. Bake cauliflower steaks for 10 minutes until tender. Remove from oven and place on a serving platter. Drizzle with sauce. Serve immediately.

8 MEXICAN FAVORITES

AS THE CHILE HARVEST MOVES FROM August to September each year, we see the brilliance of fresh green chile turn a vibrant red, eventually producing an earthy, crimson-red, dried chile. As the chiles change color their flavor evolves, bringing new and different depths of flavors to the valley with every harvest.

Fresh produce brings intense color and flavors to Mexican cuisine: fresh tomato, Hatch green and red chile, red onions, avocados, corn, and cilantro and herbs, just to name a few. Adding color through fresh garnishes, salsas, and sauces creates the best Mexican meals.

We often see a range of flavors in our Mexican fare. We hold onto authentic Mexican recipes and celebrate infused, Americanized, and vegan Mexican favorites. The basics for my Mexican recipes are beans, rice, corn, and flour tortillas; grilled meats, poultry, and fish; and creamy cheeses, lots of chile, and layers of fresh produce. We know Mexican cuisine has a rich history of being nothing short of DELICIOUS!

This collection of Mexican favorites captures the spirit and flavors of Mexican cooking we find regionally. Enjoy layers of flavor built around Hatch red and green chiles. Experience an array of authentic flavors in my Crunchy Folded Tacos, Hatch Red Chile Stacked Enchiladas, and New Mexico Christmas-Style Burritos. You can expand your palette with my Lemon Pepper Chicken Tacos and Hatch Chile Relleno Tacos, all accented with fresh produce and lots of color.

237

(*opposite page*) The abundance of Hatch chile at the annual Hatch Chile Festival on Labor Day weekend is something to see!

GRILLED CARNE ASADA TACOS

MAKES 12 SERVINGS

Carne Asada is a flavorful meat grilled and shared all along the border. Chile, citrusy juices, and tangy sauce elevate the intensity of the flavor, making it perfect for a char-grilled texture. Folding this tender meat into flour or corn tortillas creates an unforgettable taco. It makes the perfect filling for burritos and can be served as an entrée as well.

Juice of 3 limes
3 cloves garlic, minced
¼ cup olive oil
3 tbsp. soy sauce
Pinch of sugar
1 tsp. Hatch red or green chile powder (Hatch Chile Marketplace, 175)
1 jalapeño, sliced
½ cup cilantro, chopped (optional)
1 ½ lbs. beef skirt or flank steak
Twelve 6-inch flour or corn tortillas, warmed
Garnish: 2 avocados, peeled and diced; Simply Pickled Onions (90); cilantro, chopped; Hatch Mexican White Sauce (102); 2 limes, each cut into 6 wedges

1. In a medium bowl, combine lime juice, garlic, olive oil, soy sauce, sugar, and chile powder. Wisk until well blended. Add jalapeño and cilantro.

2. Add marinade and meat to a large resealable plastic bag. Work marinade through meat with your fingers. Seal plastic bag and refrigerate meat for at least 2 hours or for up to 6 hours.

3. Preheat barbecue grill to medium heat. Remove meat from marinade, discarding marinade. Grill meat for 4 to 5 minutes per side for medium rare. Remove from grill. Let stand for 6 to 8 minutes. Carve meat across the grain into thin slices, then cut into bite-size pieces.

4. To build tacos, divide meat equally among tortillas and top with avocado chunks, pickled onions, cilantro, white sauce, and lime wedges.

LEMON PEPPER CHICKEN TACOS

MAKES 8 SERVINGS

Light and lemony, this spicy chicken filling gives this taco a fresh taste. The lemon pepper seasoning adds intense flavor to this taco, making it delightfully tangy and peppery. Perfect for company but easy enough for weeknight meals.

2 tbsp. olive oil
1 clove garlic, minced
3 cups cooked chicken, shredded or diced
1 ¼ tsp. lemon pepper
1 tsp. Hatch green chile powder (Hatch Chile Marketplace, 175)
1 to 2 tbsp. fresh lemon juice
Eight 6-inch corn tortillas
2 cups mixed greens, chopped
Hatch Chile Salsa Verde (82)

1. In a medium skillet, sauté olive oil and garlic on medium-low heat for 1 to 2 minutes until garlic is softened.

2. Add chicken, lemon pepper, chile powder, and lemon juice. Increase heat to medium high and sauté until crispy and lightly charred, about 5 to 7 minutes. Remove from heat.

3. To build tacos, divide chicken equally among tortillas. Top with mixed greens and salsa. Fold tortillas in half. Serve immediately.

SPICY TURKEY TACOS WITH JALAPEÑO CRANBERRY RELISH

MAKES 6 SERVINGS

If you want a memorable, flavor-infused Thanksgiving entrée or have left-over turkey and are tired of turkey sandwiches, try these delicious tacos. Roasted turkey topped with greens, flavorful cheese, and a sweet relish makes a perfect taco.

        2 tbsp. olive oil
        3 cups roasted turkey, shredded or diced
        1 tsp. Hatch hot red chile powder (Hatch Chile Marketplace, 175)
        ¼ tsp. salt (optional)
        6-inch flour tortillas, warmed
        Cranberry Jalapeño Relish (see below)
        2 cups salad mix, chopped
        ¾ cup cotija or feta cheese, crumbled

Jalapeño Cranberry Relish
        4 jalapeños, seeded and stemmed
        2 cups fresh or frozen cranberries, divided
        1 cup cranberry sauce or jelly

1. In a small saucepan, add jalapeños and cranberries and enough water to cover berries. Bring to a boil over high heat until some of the cranberries pop and are soft, 4 to 8 minutes. Drain.

2. Add cranberry sauce or jelly and gently mash and blend over low heat. Spoon over individual tacos or cool to room temperature and transfer to an airtight container and refrigerate for least 2 hours or for up to 4 days to allow flavors to blend.

Turkey Tacos

1. In a medium skillet sauté olive oil and turkey over medium-high heat until turkey is heated through. Season with chile powder and salt and cook until crispy and slightly charred, about 4 to 8 minutes. Remove from heat.

2. To build tacos, divide turkey equally among tortillas. Top with Cranberry Jalapeño Relish, salad mix, and cheese. Fold tortillas in half and serve.

BEER-BATTERED FISH TACOS

MAKES 8 SERVINGS

These are my favorite Mexican-style fish tacos: tender fish deep-fried to a crispy golden brown, wrapped in a warm tortilla, and piled high with cabbage then drizzled with cream and fresh salsa. These tacos have so many layers of delicious flavors!

½ cup Hatch Chile Dipping Oil (99)
2 tbsp. rice vinegar
2 cups cabbage, shredded
1 cup all-purpose flour
½ tsp. baking powder
¾ cup lager beer
1 tsp. kosher salt
1 ½ lbs. skinless cod or tilapia filets
Vegetable oil
Eight 6-inch corn or flour tortillas, warmed
Hatch Mexican White Sauce (102)
Hatch Harvest Salsa (80)
2 limes, cut lengthwise into quarters

1. In a medium bowl, combine dipping oil, vinegar, and cabbage. Toss until well blended. Refrigerate for 1 to 2 hours.

2. In a large bowl, combine flour, baking powder, beer, and salt. Mix well to a thick consistency.

3. Rinse fish and pat dry with paper towel. Cut crosswise into 1-inch-wide strips.

4. Fill a deep fryer, deep heavy pot, or skillet with 2 inches of oil and heat to 350 degrees. Using tongs, dredge fish pieces in batter, shaking away excess. Gently place in oil and cook 3 to 4 pieces at a time, turning once, until golden brown, about 3 to 4 minutes per side. Drain on paper towels.

5. To build tacos, divide fish equally among the tortillas. Top with cabbage mixture, sauce, salsa, and lime wedges. Fold tortillas in half and serve.

HATCH CHILE RELLENO TACOS

MAKES 8 SERVINGS

Chile rellenos, or chile stuffed with cheese, can be messy and time consuming. I love this contemporary handheld version; flour tortillas stuffed with chile and cheese, then dipped in a light egg batter and cooked to perfection. They are so versatile, you can serve them for any meal of the day.

2 cups Hatch green chile, roasted, seeded, peeled, and chopped
2 cups Monterey Jack cheese, shredded
Eight 6-inch flour tortillas, warmed
8 eggs, lightly beaten
1 cup all-purpose flour

1. To build tacos, divide chiles and cheese equally among tortillas, placing on one half of the tortilla. Fold over and secure edges with toothpicks. Immediately place filled tortillas in a large resealable plastic bag and refrigerate 1 to 2 hours or until ready to cook.

2. Place eggs in a shallow dish. Place flour on a plate. Dip each taco in the egg mixture, coating well, then dredge in the flour on both sides. Dip the taco into egg mixture again. Place on a flat surface. Repeat with remaining tacos.

3. Spray a large skillet with cooking spray and heat over medium-high heat. Place 2 egg-dipped tacos in the skillet and cook until cheese is melted and tortilla is golden brown, 4 minutes per side. Repeat with remaining tacos. Serve immediately.

CRUNCHY FOLDED TACOS

Makes 8 servings

These Americana tacos are crispy, folded, and layered with flavor. I love this combination of red chile, meat, and creamy cheese topped with fresh produce. It is a crunchy mess but sooo good!

> 12 oz. ground beef*
> 1 tsp. cumin
> 1 tsp. Hatch Red chile powder (Hatch Chile Marketplace, 175)
> Garlic powder
> Salt and freshly ground black pepper
> 1 tbsp. flour
> 2 tbsp. water
> 8 handmade taco shells (below) or prepared shells
> 1 ½ cups lettuce, shredded
> 1 ½ cups cheddar or Monterey Jack cheese, shredded
> 1 large onion, minced
> 1 large tomato, seeded and diced

1. In a large skillet, cook ground beef until browned and cooked through, about 5 to 6 minutes. Drain excess grease.

2. Return to medium heat and add cumin, chile powder, garlic powder, salt, and pepper. Sprinkle with flour and mix well. Slowly add water and mix until well blended.

3. To build tacos, divide meat equally among taco shells, gently placing meat in the shells. Top with lettuce, cheese, and onion. Garnish with tomato chunks. Serve with a favorite salsa from my collection in chapter 3: Salsas, Sauces, and Culinary Accents.

* For chicken tacos, omit ground beef and add 2 cups shredded cooked chicken.

Homemade Taco Shells

Homemade crispy taco shells are a must. They are simple and create an authentic flavor for any taco filling.

Eight 6-inch corn tortillas
2 cups vegetable or canola oil

1. In a large heavy skillet, heat about 1 inch of oil over medium or medium-high heat to 365 degrees.

2. Using long tongs, place tortillas, one tortilla at a time, in the oil. As it starts to sizzle, flip over and fold in half with tongs. Hold until crispy. Remove and drain on paper towel. Repeat.

HATCH CHILE–INFUSED MEAT FILLINGS

The beauty of Mexican food is the simplicity of wrapping corn or flour tortillas around succulent spiced-meat fillings. Intensely flavored meats like chicken and pork are the perfect flavors to crown tostadas, roll into burritos, and fold in corn and flour tortillas for tacos. Here are a few favorites.

Pollo Verde

MAKES 2 ½ CUPS

> 1 tbsp. olive oil
> 1 clove garlic, minced
> 1 cup Hatch green chile, roasted, peeled, seeded, and chopped
> 1 onion, diced
> ¼ cup chicken broth
> 2 cups cooked chicken, diced

1. In a large skillet, heat oil over medium heat. Add garlic and cook, stirring until tender, about 1 minute. Add chiles and onion and cook, stirring until onion is translucent, 4 to 6 minutes.

2. Add broth and chicken. Mix well and simmer, stirring occasionally, until chicken is heated through, 8 to 10 minutes.

Variation: for Pollo Rojo, omit Hatch green chile and add 1 cup Hatch Red Chile Sauce (112).

Machaca Shredded Beef

MAKES 2 ½ CUPS

> 1 tbsp. vegetable oil
> 2 cloves garlic, minced

1 onion, diced

½ cup Hatch green chile, roasted, peeled, seeded, and chopped

1 medium tomato, seeded and chopped

2 cups cooked Shredded Beef (265)

⅓ cup beef broth

Juice of 2 limes

½ tsp. Hatch red or green chile powder (Hatch Chile Marketplace , 175)

Salt and freshly ground black pepper

1. In a large skillet, heat oil over medium-low heat and sauté garlic, onion, chiles, and tomato, stirring until onion is translucent, 8 to 10 minutes.

2. Add beef, beef broth, and lime juice. Increase heat to medium and cook, stirring, until all juices have evaporated, 12 to 15 minutes. Season with chile powder, salt, and pepper to taste.

Variation: For Machaca with eggs, add 2 beaten eggs to skillet after the onions are translucent. Follow the rest of the instructions.

Carne Adovada

MAKES 4 CUPS

2 to 3 lbs. boneless pork roast, cut into bite-size pieces

1 tsp. red chile flakes

1 tsp. dried oregano

1 tsp. ground cumin

1 tsp. Hatch red chile powder (Hatch Chile Marketplace, 175)

1 tsp. garlic powder

2 cups Hatch Red Chile Sauce (112)

Salt to taste

1. Place pork in a large pot. Add just enough water to cover the meat. Bring to a boil over medium-high heat. Reduce heat and boil gently,

stirring occasionally, until water and juices have evaporated, 45 minutes to 1 hour.

2. Reduce heat to low. Add chile flakes, oregano, cumin, chile powder, and garlic powder. Mix well until all spices are well coated. Add sauce, mix well, and cook until heated through.

3. Add salt to taste. If too thick, add ½ cup water. Remove from heat and serve in a bowl with a side of tortillas, in a burrito, or on a tostada.

Ground Beef, Chile, and Potatoes

MAKES 4 CUPS

2 tbsp. vegetable oil
2 large baking potatoes, peeled and diced
1 onion, minced
1 cups Hatch green chile, roasted, peeled, seeded, and chopped
12 oz. ground beef
1 tsp. salt
½ tsp. pepper

1. In a large skillet, heat oil over medium heat. Cook potatoes and onions, covered, until soft, about 12 to 14 minutes. Add green chile and cook until heated through.

2. In another skillet, cook ground beef over medium heat. Cook until meat is browned and cooked through, about 10 to 12 minutes.

3. Add the potato green chile mixture to skillet with cooked ground beef. Season and mix well.

THE ADAMS FAMILY

Scott Adams grew up on his parents' farm in Hatch, New Mexico. He continued working for them after graduating high school. In 1985 the family built an onion-packing facility and established Adams Produce, Inc. Today, thirty-eight years later, Scott, along with his wife, Terry, own and operate Adams Produce, farming over three thousand acres in the Hatch and Deming area with their growing family. Green chile and onions are their signature crops.

NEW MEXICO CHRISTMAS-STYLE BURRITOS

MAKES 4 SERVINGS

The official New Mexico state question is "Red or Green?" It's often impossible to decide, so let's do both and call it Christmas. Smothered burritos loaded with flavorful pork, beef, or chicken fillings topped with both Hatch red AND green chile sauce are a New Mexico staple. Customize your burritos to create your favorite.

> Four 10-inch tortillas, warmed
> 3-4 cups filling: Pollo Verde, Pollo Rojo, Machaca Shredded Beef, Carne Adovada, or Ground Beef, Chile, and Potatoes (248–50)
> 2 cups cheddar cheese, shredded
> 1 cup Hatch Red Chile Sauce (112), warmed
> 1 cup Hatch Green Chile Sauce (114), warmed
> Garnish: sour cream, Hatch Chile Guacamole (84), cilantro, and fresh onion slices

1. Preheat oven to 350 degrees.

2. To build burritos, divide desired meat to equally fill tortillas. Pull bottom edge of each tortilla up over the meat filling. Fold in each end of tortilla. Starting at folded bottom edge, roll up to enclose filling. Secure with a toothpick.

3. Place each burrito on individual ovenproof plate. Spoon red sauce on one end of the burrito and spoon green sauce on the other end.

4. Top each burrito equally with cheese. Place in preheated oven until cheese is melted and bubbly and burrito is heated through, 10 to 12 minutes. Remove from oven. Garnish and serve immediately.

HATCH GREEN CHILE CHICKEN ENCHILADAS

MAKES 4 TO 6 SERVINGS

These enchiladas, a New Mexico tradition, are full of a savory chicken filling and drenched in Hatch green chile sauce with its smooth complex flavor. The sauce is easy to make, and from there you just build your enchiladas, topped with cheese and garnished with fresh greens.

Vegetable oil
Twelve 6-inch corn tortillas
1 tbsp. olive oil
2 cloves garlic, minced
½ cup Hatch green chile, roasted, peeled, seeded, and chopped
1 onion, diced
¼ cup chicken broth
3 cups diced chicken, cooked*
2 cups Hatch Green Chile Sauce (114)
1 cup cheddar cheese, shredded
1 ½ cups Monterey Jack cheese, shredded
2 fresh jalapeños, sliced
1 to 2 cups fresh greens

1. Preheat oven to 350 degrees and prepare an 11 × 7 in. baking dish with cooking spray.

2. In a medium skillet, heat 1 inch oil over medium-high heat. Using tongs, carefully dip each tortilla into the oil until tortilla bubbles and is heated through, about 1 minute. Tortillas should be soft and pliable. Transfer to paper towels to drain. Repeat with remaining tortillas.

3. In a large skillet, heat olive oil over medium heat. Add garlic and cook until fragrant, about 1 minute. Add chile, onion, and broth and cook until onion is translucent, 3 to 5 minutes. Add chicken and simmer, stirring until chicken is heated through, 2 to 3 minutes.

4. Place ¼ cup chicken mixture at end of each tortilla. Roll up and place

seam-side down in baking dish. Repeat with remaining tortillas. Top rolled enchiladas with sauce and cheese.

5. Bake in preheated oven until enchiladas are heated through and cheese is melted and bubbly, 20 to 25 minutes. Garnish with jalapeños and fresh greens and serve immediately.

Variation: For Sour Cream Chicken Enchiladas, add 8 oz. sour cream to chicken mixture and mix well. Continue with remaining steps to build the enchiladas.
* You can use baked and shredded skinless chicken breast or rotisserie chicken.

HATCH RED CHILE STACKED ENCHILADAS

MAKES 4 SERVINGS

Stacked enchiladas are a New Mexico favorite. I literally prep every plate, then heat and serve them to my guests straight from the oven. Fresh corn tortillas dipped in Hatch red (or green) chile sauce and layered with onions and cheese (and whatever else you desire) bring this dish to a simplistic level of goodness.

> 3 cups Hatch Red Chile Sauce (112)
> Sixteen 6-inch corn tortillas
> 2 ½ cups cheddar and/or Monterey Jack cheese, shredded
> 2 cups fresh greens, chopped
> 1 cup cabbage, thinly shredded
> ½ cup cilantro
> 3 to 4 radishes, thinly sliced

1. Preheat oven to 375 degrees.
2. Warm sauce in a medium saucepan over low heat. Using tongs, dip tortillas, one at a time, in chile sauce, allowing excess sauce to drip off into the pan.
3. Place a tortilla on an individual ovenproof plate. Top with 1 to 2 tbsp. of additional chile sauce and 2 tbsp. cheese, then spread to the edges of each tortilla. Repeat with 3 more tortillas, placing each to create a stack with four layers per serving. Top with remaining cheese.
4. Bake in preheated oven until cheese is completely melted and heated through, 8 to 10 minutes. You can also microwave each plate on medium (50 percent) power in one-minute intervals until heated through.
5. Garnish each plate with equal amounts of cabbage, greens, cilantro, and radishes. For an additional garnish, evenly divide 2 jalapenos, thinly sliced, and/or red onion, thinly sliced.

Variations:

Beef Stacked Enchiladas: For a heartier dish, add ½ cup Hatch Ground Beef, Chile, and Potatoes (250) or Shredded Beef (265) after the second and third layer. Finish stacking with the last tortilla as directed and follow the rest of the directions.

Red Stacked Enchiladas with Veggies: For a heartier dish, add ½ cup cooked, drained black beans and ½ cup cooked, drained corn after the second and third layer. Finish stacking with the last tortilla as directed and follow the rest of the directions.

Green Stacked Enchiladas: Substitute 3 cups Hatch Green Chile Sauce (114) for Hatch Red Chile Sauce and follow the rest of the directions.

New Mexico Breakfast Enchiladas: After heating each plate of enchiladas, top the stack with an egg, cooked to order. Garnish as desired.

HATCH CHILE RELLENOS

MAKES 8 SERVINGS

Thick Hatch chiles are perfect for rellenos—stuffed with creamy cheese wrapped in a light egg batter. They are so good. This Mexican favorite takes time, but the results are amazing. You will get a bite of chile and cheese along with a golden-crusted finish. Serve these rellenos as a side dish or smothered with any of my Hatch chile sauces for a main entrée.

8 whole Hatch green chiles, roasted and peeled, stems left on
8 oz. cheddar or Monterey Jack cheese, cut into ¾-inch strips
1 cup and 1 tbsp. all-purpose flour, divided
3 large eggs, divided
1 tsp. baking powder
½ tsp. salt
Vegetable oil

1. On a cutting board, carefully slice each chile lengthwise near the stem, leaving seeds and stem. Gently stuff each chile with a slice of cheese.

2. Spread 1 cup flour on a plate. Roll stuffed chile in flour and set aside.

3. Using an electric stand mixer, beat 3 egg whites until thick and peaks are forming. Add 2 egg yolks, remaining flour, baking powder, and salt, then beat about 3 minutes (discard third egg yolk or use for another recipe). Pour egg batter into a pie pan.

4. In a deep pot or skillet, heat 3 inches of oil over medium-high heat until temperature reaches 375 degrees. Measure heat with a deep-fry thermometer.

5. Dip flour-covered chiles into egg mixture until well coated, excluding the stem, and gently place in oil to cook, 2 or 3 at a time. Fry, turning once, until golden brown, 3 to 4 minutes per side. Drain on paper towels. Serve warm.

GRILLED HATCH CHILE RELLENOS

SERVES 4 TO 6

This is slow cooking at its finest. These are crispy bacon-wrapped chiles, filled with creamy goodness. Grilling them slowly is the key to adding flavor and texture. Serve as an entrée or a side dish; they are so good.

> 6 Hatch whole green chiles, roasted and peeled
> 6 oz. Monterey Jack or queso asadero cheese, cut into ¾-inch strips
> 6 slices bacon
> 12 toothpicks, soaked in water*

1. Preheat an outdoor grill to medium heat.
2. Take each whole chile and cut a slit up the side. Place 1 piece cheese in each chile.
3. Wrap each chile with 1 piece of bacon and secure with a toothpick on each end.
4. Place wrapped chiles on grill for 4 to 6 minutes on each side, until bacon is crisp. Remove from grill and serve. Cook for 5 to 8 minutes. Slice and serve.

* Soak the toothpicks in water in order to grill the chiles without burning up on the grill.

GRAJEDA FARMS

Hatch chile is a true family affair for the Grajedas. Sergio and his family enjoy what they do: growing and selling Hatch chile. They have been farming for over twenty years in the valley and are proud to keep the Hatch traditions going. They grow an array of chile varietals, offering a full spectrum of heat levels: mild, medium, Big G, Sandia hot, Sandia Select, Barker Extra Hot, and Triple X Lumbre. You can find the Grajedas roasting and selling Hatch chile at Grajeda Farms on Highway 26 and the Hatch Chile Market in Hatch.

For more information see the Hatch Chile Marketplace (175).

Dried red chile ristras at Grajeda Farms

HATCH GREEN CHILE TAMALES

SERVES 8 TO 12

Tamales are a labor of culinary love! Warm, corn-based dough (called masa dough) filled with an intensely flavored filling is a true Mexican tradition. This meatless tamale delivers rich flavor with spicy Hatch chile and creamy cheese. These are always a treat during the holidays.

> 12 to 14 dried corn husks*
> 3 cups masa harina
> 1 tsp. baking powder
> 2 ½ cups chicken broth
> ¾ cup lard, room temperature
> 1 cup Monterey Jack cheese, grated
> 1 cup cheddar cheese, grated
> Kosher salt

1. Submerge corn husks in water until soft and pliable, about 30 minutes. Remove and dry on paper towels.

2. In a medium bowl, combine masa and baking powder. Slowly add chicken broth and lard, kneading until well blended, 3 to 5 minutes. The dough should have a thick consistency. Set aside.

3. Combine chile, cheeses, and a pinch of salt in a medium bowl. Blend well.

4. Set up your assembly area with a cutting board, corn husks, bowl of masa, and bowl of chile and cheese filling.

5. Place a damp corn husk on cutting board or work surface with the narrow end closest to you and place another corn husk overlapping along the long edges with the wide end closest to you. Place ¼ cup masa mixture in the center of overlapped husks. Spread masa into a rectangle about ¼-inch thick over both corn husks.

6. Top masa with 1 tbsp. of filling, spreading it down the center of the masa. Gently fold the right side of the corn husk toward the center, then fold the left side toward the center. Then fold the bottom end of corn husk over the cheese mixture toward the center. This may take some practice, so take it slow. Repeat with remaining corn husks.

7. In a large pot over medium-high heat, boil about 2 inches of water. Place the steam insert in the pot. Place tamales in the pot with the folded ends down, placed upright next to each other.

8. Cover and steam until dough is firm, 45 minutes to an hour. When done, the masa should pull away easily from the corn husks; it should be firm and encase the filling.

Variations:
For Green Chile Chicken Tamales, omit cheese and chile and substitute 2 cups of Pollo Verde (248).

For Green Chile Beef Tamales, omit cheese and chile and substitute 2 cups of Shredded Beef (265).

For Red Chile Pork Tamales, omit cheese and chile and substitute 2 cups of Carne Adovada (249).

* You can purchase a bag of dried corn husks in the produce or specialty section of your market or at an online retailer. Masa harina can be found in the baking section of your local market.

FIESTA TOSTADAS

MAKES 8 TOSTADAS

A tostada is so light but filling at the same time. Start with the basics: a crispy corn tortilla topped with refried beans, cheese, and lettuce. Then add extra flavor with a green chile relish and some flavorful meat and poultry fillings laced with chile. It is always messy but worth the work!

Vegetable oil
Eight 6-inch corn tortillas
2 cups refried beans, warmed*
1 cup cheddar cheese, shredded
Hatch Green Chile Relish (87)
2 cups mixed greens, chopped
1 tomato, seeded and diced
½ cup cotija cheese, crumbled

1. In a deep fryer or deep heavy pot, heat 3 inches of oil to 350 degrees. Working with one tortilla at a time, gently fry each tortilla for about 2 minutes until crispy and hard. Using tongs, carefully turn tortilla over and fry for 1 minute more. Transfer to a paper towel.

2. Place each tostada on an individual serving plate. Divide beans equally among tostada shells, spreading to the edge of each shell. Top with cheese, relish, greens, and tomato. Garnish with cotija cheese.

* For a hearty tostada, omit refried beans and add 2 cups Carne Asada (238), Pollo Verde (248), or Carne Adovada (249), warmed.

REFRIED BEANS

I use this recipe in so many of my Mexican favorites, either as part of the entrée, such as a burrito or tostada, or as a side dish. Refried beans can be made quickly. A true authentic Mexican flavor is best achieved by refrying these beans in oil. I prefer using lard for a great finishing flavor. They are delicious.

> 2 cups cooked pinto beans, drained, reserving liquid
> 2 tbsp. lard or vegetable oil*
> Salt
> Water

1. In a large skillet, heat beans and ¼ cup reserved liquid over medium-high heat. Bring to a boil for 2 minutes. Reduce heat to medium low.

2. Using a potato masher, gently mash beans. Beans should be like a thick paste. If too thick, add more reserved liquid or water, 1 tbsp. at a time, until bean mixture is easy to spread.

3. Push beans to one side of the skillet and add lard. Melt lard over medium-high heat. Gently mix beans and lard until well blended and bubbling, 4 to 6 minutes. Season with salt to taste.

* Substitute bacon drippings for lard/oil to add additional flavor.

SHREDDED BEEF

MAKES ABOUT 4 CUPS

I use shredded beef in many recipes. Customize this tender meat recipe by adding desired chile and spices or just prepare following the directions below. This recipe will create the perfect shredded beef filling for tacos, burritos, and enchiladas.

> 2 to 3 lbs. boneless beef, chuck roast, or sirloin roast
> 1 medium onion, quartered
> 3 cloves garlic, chopped
> 1 tsp. salt

1. Place roast in a large pot and fill with enough water to cover the meat by about 1 inch. Add onion and garlic and bring to a gentle boil over medium-high heat. Cover, reduce heat to medium low, and simmer until meat is tender and falling apart, 2 to 3 hours. Watch carefully, adding water if needed.

2. Remove meat and place on a cutting board. Discard broth or use in another recipe. Let meat cool for 12 to 15 minutes. Shred meat into strands with your fingers or two forks. Add salt and mix well. Let cool completely. Use immediately or place in a resealable container and refrigerate for up to 2 days or freeze for up to 3 months.

9 BREAKFAST

A relaxed weekend brunch is such a wonderful way to satisfy those breakfast cravings for some of us who don't take the time to eat breakfast during the week. Brunch is relaxing and inclusive—a way to connect with family and friends. But for many of us, breakfast is a coffee and quick bite on our way out the door. "Grab and gos" are the best for busy mornings.

This collection of recipes has variety for any type of morning. Whether you're brunching or just munching, enjoy a bite of my favorite morning fare . . . Avocado Toast infused with Hatch chile, a homemade stack of hotcakes dripping with Hatch Maple Caramel Syrup, or just a simple spicy breakfast taquito or burrito!

(*opposite page*) A brilliant sun peeking through the morning clouds over a Hatch chile field.

GREEN CHILE GRAVY

MAKES 4 SERVINGS

Gravy ladled over just about anything is delicious, but a spicy breakfast gravy is special. This family favorite is full of chunky sausage, peppery cream gravy, and Hatch green chile. Serve over flaky biscuits, fresh sourdough toast, and/or scrambled eggs.

12 oz. bulk pork sausage
1 cup Hatch green chile, roasted, peeled, seeded, and chopped
¼ cup all-purpose flour
1 ½ cups whole milk
½ cup half-and-half cream
¼ tsp. crushed red pepper flakes
½ tsp. kosher salt
1 tsp. ground black pepper

1. In a large skillet over medium heat, cook sausage until brown and cooked through. Add green chile and flour and stir until meat is coated.

2. Slowly stir in milk, half-and-half, and crushed red pepper. Cook, whisking until gravy is thick and bubbling. Add more milk if it is too thick. Season with salt and pepper. Serve immediately, garnishing with additional green chile if desired.

3. Generously ladle over fresh biscuits, sourdough toast, eggs, and/or sausage patties.

BREAKFAST ROLLED TACOS

MAKES 12 TACOS

These taquitos are so good! They are not typically served for breakfast, but these sausage-filled taquitos are salty, crispy, spicy, and perfect with eggs in the morning. Take them as a "grab and go" or simply as a side dish for eggs.

12 oz. breakfast sausage*
½ cup Hatch green chile, roasted, peeled, seeded, and minced
12 corn tortillas, warmed
Oil

1. In a large skillet, cook sausage slowly over medium-low heat, breaking up and keeping the browned pieces in very small crumbles. Add chile and mix well.

2. To build taquitos, place 2 tbsp. of sausage mixture at one end of each

tortilla. Gently roll tortilla and secure with a toothpick. Place taquitos in a resealable plastic bag to keep moist. Refrigerate for up to 2 days until ready to cook.

3. To cook, fill deep skillet or heavy pot with 3 inches of oil and heat to 350 degrees. Using tongs, gently place 3 to 4 taquitos at a time in the hot oil and cook, turning once, until golden brown and crispy, 2 to 3 minutes. Drain on paper towels. Lightly season with salt.

* I use Jimmy Dean's sausage for the added spices. Find a favorite breakfast sausage or use ground beef.

MIGAS AND PAPPAS

MAKES 8 SERVINGS

This special dish will entice your morning tastebuds. It has just a little bit of everything: potatoes, chile, tortillas, and eggs. Yum! It is crazy but tasty, a breakfast menagerie.

> 4 tbsp. vegetable or canola oil, divided
> 3 to 4 corn tortillas strips, cut into ½-inch strips
> 1 baked potato, diced into ¼-inch cubes
> 1 small onion, diced
> 3 Hatch green chiles, roasted, peeled, seeded, and chopped
> 2 cloves garlic, minced
> 8 eggs, whipped
> 2 tsp. Hatch red chile powder (Hatch Chile Marketplace, 175) (optional)
> ½ tsp. salt
> 1 cup Monterey Jack cheese, grated
> ½ cup cotija cheese, crumbled
> ¼ cup cilantro, minced
> 2 avocados, peeled and sliced

1. Heat 2 tbsp. of oil in a skillet over medium-high heat. Once hot, add tortilla strips and cook until crispy and golden brown. Remove with a slotted spoon and drain on paper towels.

2. Add diced potato to the skillet and cook over medium-high heat until lightly browned and crispy. Remove with a slotted spoon and drain on paper towels.

3. Add remaining oil to skillet and sauté onion and chile until onion is soft, then add garlic and cook until onion is transparent, about 4 to 6 minutes.

4. Combine eggs, chile powder, and salt in a mixing bowl. Reduce heat in the skillet to medium and add eggs to the onion mixture.

5. Cook and stir egg mixture until it starts to firm up. Fold in Monterey Jack cheese, tortilla strips, and potatoes. Cook until eggs are cooked through, about 6 to 8 minutes.

6. Transfer eggs to a serving platter and garnish with cotija cheese, cilantro, and avocado slices. Serve immediately.

BIAD CHILI COMPANY

Don Biad, brother of Tessie Biad Franzoy, came to the Hatch Valley in the early 1950s. He began growing green and red chile with his two sons.

Today, the Biad family has expanded their operations to produce various forms of dehydrated red chile, paprika, green chili, and green jalapeño. The company also breeds its own seed lines and specializes in original New Mexico chile pepper varieties, including "heritage" varieties. Now in its third generation, the Biad family operates three dehydration facilities in New Mexico and Texas as well as a paprika oleoresin extraction facility in the Mesilla Valley of New Mexico.

HATCH HASH

Makes 6 servings

Skillet-fried potatoes, vegetables, and meat—that's hash! Add chile and that's Hatch Hash! Start with a favorite cooked meat, even leftovers . . . then add freshness and depth with lots of veggies. You will love it. Serve with eggs, toast, or just by itself with more chile!

> 2 tbsp. vegetable or canola oil
> 2 cloves garlic, minced
> 1 onion, diced
> 1 red bell pepper, cored, seeded, and chopped
> 1 cup Hatch green chile, roasted, peeled, seeded, and chopped
> 3 cups gold potatoes, diced and fried
> 2 cups cooked corn beef, roasted pork, or beef, shredded or cubed
> 1 tsp. salt
> Ground black pepper
> 1 tsp. flat parsley, minced

1. Heat a heavy skillet over medium heat, add oil, and sauté garlic, onions, bell pepper, and green chile until soft and onions are transparent. Cook until slightly browned, stirring.

2. Add cooked potatoes, meat, and spices. Cook over medium-high heat, pressing down with a spatula until potatoes are browned, then flip. Repeat until hash is crispy and cooked through. Serve immediately.

SPICY AVOCADO TOAST

Fresh avocado slathered on sourdough toast is heaven. But add a drizzle of chile-infused oil and you have a breakfast hit on your hands. Garnish with crispy bacon and a tomato slice for a heartier bite. Simplicity!

    4 slices sourdough bread
    3 tbsp. Hatch Chile Dipping Oil (99), divided
    2 avocados
    1 tsp. red chile flakes, divided
    1 tsp. salt
    Ground pepper
    2 green onions, greens only

1. Preheat oven to 350 degrees.

2. Lightly brush one side of each piece of bread with dipping oil. Place on a baking sheet (oil side up) and toast until golden brown, about 4 to 6 minutes. Place on individual plates.

3. Peel, remove seed, and dice avocados, then place in a medium bowl. Add ½ tsp. chile flakes, salt, and a pinch of pepper and mash to desired consistency.

4. Divide avocado mixture evenly on toasted bread. Top with onions and remaining chile flakes.

5. Lightly drizzle each piece of toast with remaining dipping oil.

Variation: For a Spicy Bacon and Tomato Avocado toast, garnish evenly with 4 pieces of bacon, cooked and crumbled, and 1 large tomato sliced into 8 thin slices.

HATCH EGG MUFFIN

MAKES 4 SERVINGS

Grab and gos are great when you're on the run, and this breakfast sandwich does the trick. Stacked high with fresh eggs, melted cheese, and spicy chile, it is a true delight when you can relax and enjoy it. A great way to start the day.

> 4 English muffins
> 1 cup Hatch Green Taco Sauce (86)
> 4 slices ham, ¼-inch thick*
> 1 cup Hatch green chile, roasted, peeled, seeded, and chopped
> 1 tbsp. butter
> 4 eggs, whipped
> 1 cup cheddar cheese, grated, or 4 slices of American cheese

1. Preheat oven to 200 degrees.

2. Toast English muffins to desired crispiness.

3. Spread taco sauce on the bottom of each toasted English muffin. Set aside.

4. In a skillet, cook ham slices over medium heat until lightly browned and heated through. Place on top of English muffin bottoms and top with equal amounts of green chile.

5. In a skillet, melt butter over medium heat. Cook eggs over medium heat until firm and fluffy. Remove from skillet and divide evenly among muffins. Top with equal amounts of cheese. Place muffin top on cheese.

6. Place muffins in oven to keep warm and melt cheese until ready to serve.

* I often serve these with 4 slices of thick maple bacon, cooked and cut in half for each muffin.

HANGOVER BURRITO

MAKES 4 SERVINGS

A few years back while in the restaurant business, I created this breakfast burrito for our Saturday and Sunday morning diners and it became a favorite. Hot Hatch green chile, bacon, egg, and chorizo sausage hits the spot after a late night out! Take it as a "grab and go" or enjoy it smothered in a rich creamy chile sauce.

 2 tbsp. oil
 8 eggs, slightly beaten
 1 cup hot Hatch green chile, roasted, peeled, seeded, and chopped
 5 oz. chorizo sausage, cooked and crumbled
 8 strips thick bacon, cooked and crumbled
 Eight 10-inch flour tortillas, warmed
 1 ½ cups cheddar cheese, grated
 Cheesy Green Chile Sauce (114), warmed

1. Heat the oil in a large skillet over medium heat. Add eggs and cook, stirring until slightly firm. Add chile, cooked chorizo sausage, and bacon to the eggs. Continue cooking and stirring until eggs are cooked and firm. Remove skillet from heat.

2. Divide eggs evenly among tortillas by scooping egg mixture on one edge of each tortilla. Top with equal amounts of cheese and roll into a burrito, tucking in each open end. Place each burrito seam-side down in foil (and wrap to go), or place on a plate and top with warmed chile sauce. Serve immediately.

RED CHILE CHILAQUILES

MAKES 4 SERVINGS

Combining a salsa and a smooth chile sauce brings an infectious level of heat to the texture of crispy corn tortilla chips. Top this breakfast special with a fried egg if you like, but I like mine without! Either way, lots of fresh garnish finishes it off with flavor.

　　1 cup Hatch Harvest Salsa (80)
　　1 cup Hatch Red Chile Sauce (112)
　　24 fresh-fried or store-bought corn tortilla chips
　　¾ cup cheddar or Monterey Jack cheese, shredded
　　1 tbsp. cilantro, minced
　　3 green onions, minced
　　1 medium red onion, thinly sliced
　　1 avocado, cored, peeled, and diced
　　¼ cup cotija cheese, crumbled

1. In a large skillet, combine salsa and chile sauce over medium heat. Reduce heat to medium low and simmer until heated through.

2. Slowly fold in the tortilla chips, stirring until soft and coated with sauce and bubbly, about 6 to 8 minutes. Top with cheese.

3. Once cheese has melted remove from heat and top with cilantro, onions, avocado, and cotija cheese. Serve immediately.

Variation: For a full Hatch red chile flavor, omit the salsa and increase the Hatch Red Chile Sauce by 1 cup.

HUEVOS RANCHEROS

MAKES 4 SERVINGS

This traditional ranch-style breakfast is a favorite, with Hatch chile sauces and salsas. It is a full plate of eggs and corn tortillas smothered with chile goodness. Serve with a side of fried potatoes, black beans, or refried beans for a plentiful breakfast.

> 3 tbsp. oil
> Eight 6-inch corn tortillas
> 2 cups Hatch Red Chile Sauce (112) or Hatch Green Chile Sauce (114),* warmed
> 8 eggs
> 1 cup cheddar or Monterey Jack cheese, grated

1. Preheat oven to 200 degrees. Place ovenproof serving plates in preheated oven to warm.

2. In a large skillet over medium-high heat, add oil and heat for 1 minute. Using tongs, carefully dip each tortilla into the oil until tortilla bubbles and is heated through, about 1 minute. Transfer to paper towels to drain. Repeat with remaining tortillas.

3. Carefully remove warmed plates from oven and place 2 tortillas slightly overlapping each other on each warmed plate. Return to oven.

4. In a skillet, scramble or fry eggs separately, as desired.

5. Again, carefully remove warmed plates from oven and place 2 cooked eggs on top of tortillas on each plate and smother with equal amounts of chile sauce. Garnish with equal amounts of cheese. Return to oven until cheese is melted, 3 to 4 minutes. Serve immediately.

* Huevos Rancheros is a dish that can be customized for any palette. For a fresh salsa-flavored sauce, substitute 2 cups Hatch Harvest Salsa (80), warmed, for green or red chile sauces.

CHILE FANATICS

Jesus and Andrea Soto, Hatch farmers, have been growing chile since 1998. They started out wholesaling chile and specializing in handmade chile ristras. Mrs. Soto taught her children how to craft strings of red chiles and developed a new method of ristra construction that was more durable and long-lasting, which increased their business regionally.

Eventually, the Sotos started retailing Hatch chile products, ranging from green and red chile pods, chile ristras, powders, salsas, and chile brittle to pinto beans and home décor.

Today, they welcome visitors from around the world to their shop on Hall Street in Hatch, New Mexico.

For more information see the Hatch Chile Marketplace (175).

CHILE HAM BREAKFAST PIE

MAKES 6 TO 8 SERVINGS

This breakfast pie is light—almost a crustless quiche-style entrée—but filling. Cheesy chile layers intertwined in a tasty way with savory ham creates a perfect starter for your weekend.

¼ cup butter
4 slices sourdough bread
1 cup cubed ham, fully cooked
⅔ cup Hatch green chile, roasted, peeled, seeded, and chopped
2 ½ cups cheddar cheeses, shredded and divided
8 eggs
1 cup whole or 2 percent milk
¼ tsp. garlic powder
¼ tsp. salt
Pinch of black ground pepper
½ cup Hatch Chile Salsa Verde (82)

1. Coat a glass pie plate with cooking spray.

2. Butter each piece of bread, then cut into cubes for a single layer and place at the bottom of the deep-dish pie plate. Top with ham, green chile, and 1 ¾ cups cheese.

3. In a medium bowl, whisk together eggs, milk, garlic powder, salt, and pepper. Pour over bread cubes and ham mixture, cover with foil, and refrigerate overnight.

4. When ready to bake, preheat oven to 350 degrees.

5. Remove egg dish from the refrigerator. Keep covered with foil. Bake for 30 minutes. Uncover and top with remaining cheese. Bake for another 12 to 15 minutes. Insert knife: it is done when the knife comes out clean. Let sit for 5 to 7 minutes. Cut in pie slices and serve on individual plates. Drizzle each slice with equal amounts of salsa and serve immediately.

HATCH EGGS BENEDICT

MAKES 4 SERVINGS

Upscale brunch delights are such a breakfast treat. Adding a little kick—a Hatch twist—to this American classic adds a spicy flavor and some heat. Red chile powder laces the creamy, rich, egg-based sauce, making it distinctive and delicious.

> 2 egg yolks
> 2 tsp. water
> 1½ sticks butter, melted and cooled
> 1½ tsp. fresh lemon juice
> ½ tsp. Hatch red chile powder, divided (Hatch Chile Marketplace, 175)
> 4 pieces Canadian Bacon
> 2 English muffins, split
> 4 tbsp. Hatch Red Chile sauce (112)
> 4 fresh eggs, divided
> 4 tbsp. vinegar
> ½ tsp. salt
> 1 tsp. chives, minced
> Hollandaise Sauce (see below)

Hollandaise Sauce

> Place 2 egg yolks plus 2 tsp. water in a blender. Set egg whites aside for another recipe. Blend on low, and very slowly pour melted butter into eggs. Add lemon juice and red chile powder. Blend 1 minute, then transfer to a small saucepan. Cook over low heat, whisking constantly until sauce thickens, about 2 minutes. If the sauce gets too thick, add another ½ tsp. water. Transfer to a small bowl and place plastic wrap directly on sauce to cover and keep warm.

Eggs Benedict

1. In a medium skillet, cook Canadian bacon over medium heat until heated through. Set aside.

2. Toast English muffin halves until golden brown. Spread each slice with 1 tbsp. red chile sauce.

3. Poach eggs by filling a saucepan with water. Bring water to a simmer, not a boil. Add 1 tbsp. of vinegar. Using a spoon, create a swirl or vortex in the water. Gently drop one egg in the middle of the water. Allow the egg to cook until white is firm, 4 to 5 minutes. Repeat with remaining eggs and vinegar.

4. To build each eggs benedict, place one slice of Canadian bacon on each open-faced English muffin bottom. Top with 1 poached egg and warm hollandaise sauce. Garnish with a dash of salt and chives and serve immediately.

SPICY SWEET CINNAMON ROLLS

MAKES 6 TO 10 ROLLS

This classic and traditional breakfast bun is laced with a hint of red chile. It's a homestyle cinnamon roll that will satisfy those cravings for rich sweetness any morning. These buttery rolls take some time but are worth it, so plan ahead.

Roll Ingredients

1 (standard) packet active dry yeast
1 tbsp. granulated sugar
¾ cup warm water
2 cups all-purpose flour
1 tbsp. vegetable oil
½ tsp. salt
⅓ cup butter, melted
1 cup white granulated sugar
½ cup brown sugar
1 ½ tbsp. cinnamon

Icing Ingredients

2 cups powdered sugar
½ tsp. Hatch red chile powder (Hatch Chile Marketplace, 175)
Pinch of salt
¼ cup melted butter
3 tbsp. half-and-half cream
1 tsp. vanilla

Cinnamon Roll

1. Place yeast and sugar in the bowl of a stand mixer with a dough hook. Add very warm water and whisk until blended, then cover and allow to sit for 5 to 7 minutes.

2. Slowly add flour, oil, and salt. Mix on low until blended and stringy, about 3 to 4 minutes.

3. Remove from bowl and knead with hands on a lightly floured surface for 2 to 3 minutes. Place in a greased bowl and cover for 1 hour at room temperature.

4. While the dough rests, make the cinnamon filling. In a medium bowl mix together melted butter, sugars, and cinnamon. Set aside.

5. Punch the dough down and then roll out onto a floured surface in a long rectangle shape. You want the dough to be thin, ¼ inches high.

6. Sprinkle sugar mixture across dough evenly.

7. Carefully and slowly roll the longest end into a tight roll, creating a tight log.

8. With a sharp knife cut the dough into ½-inch slices. Place in a lightly greased cast-iron skillet or round baking dish. Do not overcrowd. Cover with a kitchen towel and let rise until doubled in size, 60 to 90 minutes.

9. Bake until lightly browned, 15 to 25 minutes.

Icing

1. To make the icing, combine powdered sugar, chile powder, and salt in a medium bowl. Slowly add melted butter, half-and-half, and vanilla, mixing until well blended.

2. The icing consistency should be very spreadable. Spread on warm rolls. Lightly sprinkle additional chile powder for more heat.

Variation: For a spicier cinnamon roll, add 1 tsp. of Hatch red chile powder to the cinnamon filling in step 4.

HOTCAKES WITH HATCH MAPLE CARAMEL SYRUP

MAKES 4 TO 6 SERVINGS

Easy homemade pancakes are a foundational breakfast favorite. I love the unexpected hint of chile at the end of every bite. The caramelized syrup is a treat: rich, warm, and drizzly, it melts the butter as it seeps into each little cake with a zest of chile flavor.

Hotcakes

2 cups all-purpose flour

2 tsp. baking powder

½ tsp. Hatch Red chile powder (Hatch Chile Marketplace, 175)

¼ tsp. salt

2 ½ tbsp. sugar

2 eggs

1 ¾ cups milk

¼ cup melted butter

1. Combine flour, baking powder, chile powder, salt, and sugar in a large bowl.

2. Whisk eggs and milk together in a small bowl.

3. Slowly add egg mixture to the flour mixture. Mix until smooth while slowly drizzling butter into batter.

4. Heat a skillet or griddle, lightly coated with cooking spray, over medium heat. Spoon 3 to 4 tbsp. of the batter onto the skillet for each pancake. Brown on both sides and serve hot.

Hatch Caramel Maple Syrup

1 cup pure maple syrup

¼ tsp. salt

1 tsp. Hatch red chile powder (Hatch Chile Marketplace, 175)

2 tbsp. butter

¼ cup heavy cream

1. Add syrup to a small pot and bring to a slow boil over medium heat, about 10 to 15 minutes. Using a candy thermometer, remove from heat once syrup gets to 250–270 degrees.

2. Add salt and chile powder, butter, and cream, whisking constantly for about 2 minutes.

3. Syrup will thicken as it cools. Keep warm on low heat and serve immediately.

10 DESSERTS

SWEET PLEASURES CAN BE FOUND IN the little things, like an afternoon walk, wandering through the village of Hatch, strolling around the local shops, stopping in at the local museum, or grabbing a ristra or jar of chile at the Hatch Chile Express. If you're looking for a sweet spot, stop in for a green chile lemonade or a creamy ice cream shake at Sparky's, always a favorite.

Most of us have a passion for sweets . . . just a bite, a spoonful, or a slice of sweetness. After indulging in all of this savory chile fare, we can't forget our sweets. So I have created sweet delicacies with a hint of chile. Honestly, I rarely ever turn down dessert. Even just a bite finishes any meal with pleasure. You'll find my favorite desserts and sweet treats in this collection. Enjoy a taste of Spicy Bananas Flambé, rich caramel sauce wrapped around sautéed bananas, or a bite of Creamy Mexican Chocolate Fudge loaded with pecans. During the warmer months try my Grilled Pineapple Pound Cake, full of fresh flavors. These recipes showcase seasonal fruits and chile, chocolate, and nuts that are spiced up and delicious. They are rich and full of heat. I hope you love them too!

289

(*opposite page*) Sweet nostalgia on top of Sparky's Burgers, Barbeque, and Espresso.

SPICY BANANAS FLAMBÉ

MAKES 4 SERVINGS

This elegant dessert is fun and exciting. The rich caramel sauce spiked with rum and chile is a sweet backdrop for warm bananas and cool vanilla ice cream. Flame it up for a little drama and enjoy!

> 4 tbsp. butter
> ¼ cup granulated sugar
> ¼ cup dark brown sugar
> Pinch of cinnamon
> ½ tsp. Hatch red chile pepper (Hatch Chile Marketplace, 175)
> 4 oz. white rum
> 2 bananas, sliced lengthwise and then in half, creating 8 pieces
> 1 qt. premium vanilla ice cream

1. In a heavy medium skillet, melt butter over medium-high heat. Add sugars, cinnamon, and chile. Cook, stirring constantly, until sugar is dissolved, about 4 to 5 minutes.

2. Add banana slices and sauté until soft, about 2 to 3 minutes.

3. Remove from heat. Drizzle rum over banana mixture and immediately ignite the alcohol, using a long lighter to create low flames.

4. Gently shake the skillet around to baste the bananas until the flame burns off.

5. Add 3 to 4 scoops of ice cream to the skillet and serve immediately.

CHILE PEPPER INSTITUTE

I often stop by the little shop at the Chile Pepper Institute (CPI) at New Mexico State University to pick up a "chile" gift, such as chile cookbooks, chile seeds, posters, aprons, etc. They also offer salsas, sauces, and frozen and dried chile. This nonprofit organization supports the chile industry through research and education. You can find lots of information about various chiles, Hatch chile, and Hatch chile products through their website.

Established in 1992, CPI continues to build on the research of the famous horticulturist Fabian Garcia (the father of the US chile pepper industry). Garcia began standardizing chile pepper varieties in the early 1900s at New Mexico College of Agriculture and Mechanical Arts, now known as NMSU, changing New Mexico agriculture. Most recently, Garcia was inducted into the Agricultural Hall of Fame.

www. cpi.nmsu.edu

CHILE APPLE CHIMICHANGAS

MAKES 4 SERVINGS

These crispy flour tortillas are filled with sweet apple and green chile, a combination where the ingredients complement each other in a special way. Chimichangas are so easy to make and loved by so many. These apple tarts can be served for breakfast or dessert.

2 large apples, cored and chopped
1 cup Hatch green chile, roasted, peeled, seeded, and chopped
½ cup granulated sugar, divided
1 ½ tsp. ground cinnamon, divided
1 tsp. fresh lemon juice
¼ cup water
Four 10-inch flour tortillas, warmed
Oil

1. In a medium bowl, combine apples, chile, ¼ cup sugar, ½ tsp. cinnamon, lemon juice, and water. Let stand at room temperature for 15 minutes. Combine remaining sugar and cinnamon in a small bowl and set aside.

2. Pour apple mixture into a medium saucepan over medium-high heat. Bring to a boil and cook until the apples are soft and cooked down, about 10 to 12 minutes. Remove from heat and cool at room temperature.

3. To build the chimichangas, pile 2 heaping tbsps. of apple filling on one end of the tortilla, then fold sides of tortilla over the filling. Roll the tortilla up and secure with a toothpick. Repeat with remaining tortillas and filling. Place in a resealable bag and chill in refrigerator for 1 hour or up to 2 days.

4. To cook, fill a deep skillet or fryer with 3 inches of oil and heat to 350 degrees. Using long tongs, gently place 1 to 2 chimichangas in the hot oil and deep fry, turning once until crisp and golden brown, about 2 to 3 minutes per side. Remove and place on paper towel. Dust with remaining cinnamon sugar. Garnish and serve immediately.

CHILE PECAN BRITTLE

MAKES 4 TO 6 SERVINGS

Crispy, sweet brittle with a kick of chile creates a delicious candy but also a topping for an ice cream sundae or garnish for an apple pie. Perfect for a gift from the kitchen . . .

1 cup granulated sugar
1 cup light corn syrup
½ cup water
½ tsp. salt
1 ½ tsp. Hatch hot chile powder (Hatch Chile Marketplace, 175)
1 ¼ cups pecan pieces
½ tbsp. butter
1 tbsp. baking powder

1. Prepare a baking sheet with cooking spray.

2. In a large saucepan, combine sugar and corn syrup over medium-high heat.

3. Add water, salt, and chile powder. Stirring constantly, cook until candy thermometer reaches 300 degrees. Continue stirring for 1 minute.

4. Remove pan from heat and stir in pecans. Stir in butter until melted. Add baking soda and stir immediately as it foams until well blended.

5. Quickly pour and spread mixture onto baking sheet. Cool for 1 to 2 hours.

6. Break into pieces.

GRILLED PINEAPPLE POUND CAKE

MAKES 6 SERVINGS

Light grill marks add interest and flavor to the foundation of this dessert: slices of rich pound cake. This dessert features fresh fruit glazed with a light syrup and crowned with a chile-infused sweet coconut. Perfect for a midday gathering or family barbeque.

> ¾ cup sweetened coconut flakes
> 1 tsp. Hatch red or green chile powder (Hatch Chile Marketplace, 175)
> 6 slices butter pound cake*
> 6 pineapple slices, drained
> 4 to 6 strawberries, cored and sliced
> 3 kiwis, peeled and sliced
> ¼ cup light corn syrup
> 2 tbsp. fresh lime juice

1. Preheat grill to medium heat.

2. In a small bowl, combine coconut with chile powder. Set aside.

3. Grill slices of pound cake and pineapple slices lightly over medium heat, about 3 minutes per side. Set aside.

4. In a medium bowl, gently combine strawberries and kiwi with the light corn syrup and the lime juice.

5. Place 1 piece of grilled cake on each serving plate. Top with grilled pineapple slices. Spoon strawberry mixture evenly over the top of each slice. Garnish with chile coconut and serve.

* Use a favorite pound cake or angel food recipe for a homemade cake. I typically make this dessert when I am pressed for time, so I will pick up a prepared angel food or pound cake at the market.

VILLAGE MARKET

Art Alba can tell you just about all you want to know about Hatch chile and chile products, including who grows them and who processes them. He does so every day as he oversees the daily operation at the Village Market, the local grocery store in Hatch. He and partners Vicki and Chuck Watkins take great care in offering an amazing variety of Hatch chile products for the community.

"The credit should be given to the local venders and processors of chile products," says Art. "They all run a first-class processing operation. We want to support them and offer our customers the best chile products. We sell award-winning salsas, like the Bossy Gourmet brand; best sellers like the Hatch Chile label by Jimmy and Jo Lytle; and Chile Fanatics by the Sotos family. Every local product does so well."

Village Market also offers private-label jellies, jams, and sauces along with local honey, flour, pinto beans, chips, dried chile pods, and corn husks. Their Mexican breads and deli specialties have a local flavor. On Fridays they offer red and green enchiladas, and their smoked meats are offered daily, all on a first-come-first-served basis due to popularity.

For more information see the Hatch Chile Marketplace (175).

297

CREAMY MEXICAN CHOCOLATE FUDGE

MAKES 10 TO 12 SERVINGS

Chocolate fudge is a must during the holidays at my house. I just love the rich and chocolatey goodness of this recipe. It is laced with cinnamon and chile, which reminds me of Mexican chocolate. It makes a sweet gift from the kitchen any time of year.

> ¾ cup butter
> ⅔ cup evaporated milk
> 3 cups white sugar
> 2 tsp. cinnamon
> 2 tsp. Hatch red chile powder (Hatch Chile Marketplace, 175)
> One 7-oz. jar of marshmallow cream
> 1 ½ cups semisweet chocolate chips
> 1 tsp. vanilla
> 1 cup pecans, chopped*

1. Prepare a glass baking dish by coating with butter; use a 10 × 10 in. dish for thicker fudge or a 7 × 11 in. dish for a thinner fudge.

2. In a large, heavy saucepan, melt butter over medium heat. Add evaporated milk, sugar, cinnamon, and chile powder, then stir with a long wooden spoon until dissolved in butter. Scrape all sugar crystals on the side of the pot into the butter. Stir until sugar is dissolved.

3. Bring sugar mixture to a full boil for 4 to 5 minutes or until candy thermometer reaches 234 to 236 degrees. Remove saucepan from heat.

4. Working quickly, remove lid and paper seal from marshmallow cream jar. Microwave marshmallow cream on medium heat for 10 to 15 seconds to make it easier to add to the sugar mixture.

5. Alternately stir in chocolate chips and warmed marshmallow cream. Blend until smooth.

6. Fold in vanilla and pecans, stirring until smooth.

7. Pour into the baking dish and allow to cool at room temperature for at least 3 hours or overnight. Cut and serve.

* For toasted pecans, spread pecans out on a baking sheet and bake at 200 degrees for 4 to 5 minutes, just until they become fragrant.

CHILE-DUSTED CHURROS

MAKES 6 TO 8 SERVINGS (12 TO 14 CHURROS)

Sweet and simple churros are a favorite Mexican dessert. I have taken this simple, fried, and sugared dough and spiced it up in a Hatch kind of way, creating a melt-in-your-mouth experience.

> 1 cup and 2 tbsp. granulated sugar, divided
> 2 tsp. ground cinnamon
> 1½ tsp. Hatch red chile powder, divided (Hatch Chile Marketplace, 175)
> 1 tsp. kosher salt, divided
> 1 cup water
> 2 tbsp. shortening
> 1 cup all-purpose flour
> 1 tsp. vanilla
> Oil
> 1 cup Sweet Caramel Chile Sauce (118)

1. Combine 1 cup of sugar, cinnamon, 1 tsp. chile powder, and ½ tsp. kosher salt and spread on a plate or flat surface. Set aside.

2. In a medium saucepan, combine water, shortening, 2 tbsp. sugar, and ½ tsp. salt. Bring to a boil over high heat. Boil, stirring, for 1 minute. Remove from heat and add flour, stirring until mixture forms a soft dough ball.

3. Transfer dough to a bowl. Add vanilla. Mix well and let cool.

4. Fill a deep fryer, deep heavy pot, or deep skillet with 3 inches of oil and heat to 350 degrees, checking with a candy or deep-fry thermometer.

5. Place dough into cookie press* and carefully press out 4-inch-long churros into hot oil.

6. Using tongs, gently fry 3 to 4 churros at a time, turning once, until golden brown and crispy on the ends and a bit soft in the middle, 2 to 3 minutes.

7. Using a slotted spoon, transfer to a baking sheet lined with paper towels to drain.

8. Roll warm churros in cinnamon mixture until they are well coated. Serve warm with a bowl of Sweet Caramel Chile Sauce (118).

* Use a cookie press with a ⅜-inch tip or a pastry bag with a ⅜-inch star tip. Check for doneness in the center. Churros should be soft in the center but not doughy.

MEXICAN CHOCOLATE PECAN PIE

MAKES 6 SERVINGS

I have always enjoyed this gooey, chocolatey pecan pie. Adding just a hint of chile at the end of every bite elevates the flavors in a very special way. The chocolate, chile, and cinnamon combination adds depth to this traditional pecan pie.

> ¼ cup butter, softened
> ½ cup granulated sugar
> 2 tsp. Hatch red chile powder (Hatch Chile Marketplace, 175)
> Pinch of cayenne
> 1 tsp. ground cinnamon
> 3 eggs
> 1 cup dark corn syrup
> 6 oz. semisweet chocolate, coarsely chopped
> 2 cups pecans, coarsely chopped
> One 9-inch unbaked pie crust*

1. Preheat oven to 350 degrees.

2. In a large bowl, using a stand mixer, gently combine butter, sugar, red chile powder, cayenne powder, and cinnamon on medium speed. Slowly beat in eggs and corn syrup. Remove from mixer and fold in chocolate pieces and pecans, mixing by hand.

3. Pour pecan mixture into unbaked pie crust. Cover the edges of the pie crust with foil to keep from overcooking the edges of crust.

4. Bake pie in preheated oven for 10 minutes. Reduce oven temperature to 300 degrees and bake until the crust is slightly browned and the filling is firmly set, 35 to 40 minutes. Let cool completely on a wire rack.

* When pressed for time, I use a store-bought pie crust, following directions and covering the crimped edges with foil to keep from overcooking. It will work with your favorite homemade pie crust as well.

INDEX

303

Onion Flatbread, 204; Chile Cheese Crisp, 54; Chile Garlic Toast, 147, *147*; Chile Ham Breakfast Pie, 281; Chile Relleno Black Bean Bake, 234; Chile-Rubbed Ribeye, 210, *210*; Crispy Chicken Chile Sandwich, *194*, *195*; Crispy Hatch Chile Cheese Bites, 47; Crunchy Folded Tacos, 246–47; Duane Gillis's Steak and Chile Medallions, 211; Fiesta Tostadas, 263; Green Chile Cheese Bread, 148; Green Chile Chicken Enchilada Flatbread, 205; Green Chile Lasagna, 216–17, *217*; Grilled Hatch Chile Rellenos, 259; Hatch Chile Cheese Puff, 73; Hatch Chile Mac and Cheese, 136–37, *137*; Hatch Chile Nachos, 66; Hatch Chile Pecan Cheese Roll, 42, *43*; Hatch Chile Potato Skins, 63; Hatch Chile Rellenos, 258; Hatch Chile Relleno Tacos, 245; Hatch Chile Stuffed Mushrooms, 58; Hatch Chile Verde con Queso, 50; Hatch Chile Wontons, 62; Hatch Egg Muffin, 274, *275*; Hatch Garden Fresh Flatbread, 204; Hatch Green and Red Chile Fries, 38–39; Hatch Green Chile Cheeseburger, 184–85, *184*, *185*, *187*; Hatch Green

Chile Chicken Enchiladas, 254–55, *255*; Hatch Green Chile Corn Bread, 146; Hatch Green Chile Tamales, 261–62; Hatch Pimento Spread, 40; Hatch Quick Queso, 51, *51*; Hatch Red Chile Stacked Enchiladas, 256–57, *257*; Hatch Red Honey Chicken Quesadilla, 55; Hatch Scalloped Skillet Potatoes, *138*, *139*; Hot Honey and Lemon Flatbread, 205; Huevos Rancheros, 279; Loaded Hatch Baked Potatoes, 142–43, *143*; Migas and Pappas, 270; Pesto Sausage Flatbread, 204; Red Chile Chilaquiles, 278; Red Chile Refried Bean Mash, 46; Red Chile Sausage Ziti, 220, *221*; Savory Chile Cheesecake, 68, *69*; Spicy Turkey Tacos with Jalapeño Cranberry Relish, 242–43, *243*. *See also* blue cheese; cotija cheese; cream cheese; Parmesan cheese; provolone cheese; ricotta cheese; Swiss cheese
Cheesy Green Chile Sauce, 111; Hangover Burrito, 276, *277*
Cheesy White Bean Red Chile Bake, 231
chicken: Chicken Tortilla Soup, 172, *173*; Crispy Chicken Chile Sandwich, *194*, *195*; Green Chile Chicken Alfredo, 214, *215*; Green

Chile Chicken Chowder, 168; Green Chile Chicken Enchilada Flatbread, 205; Hatch Chicken Salad Sandwich, 198; Hatch Chile Chicken Lettuce Wraps, 64, *65*; Hatch Chile Chicken Posole, 164; Hatch Chile Chicken Salad, 128; Hatch Chile Chicken Sliders, 56–57, *57*; Hatch Chile Nachos, 66; Hatch Chile Skillet Chicken, 213, *213*; Hatch Cobb Salad, *130*, 131; Hatch Green Chile Chicken Enchiladas, 254–55, *255*; Hatch-Style Gumbo, 166–67; Lemon Pepper Chicken Tacos, 240, *241*; Pollo Verde, 248; Roasted Chicken with Lemon Chile Glaze, 218
Chile and Caramelized Onion Flatbread, 204
Chile Apple Chimichangas, 292–93, *293*
Chile Avocado Salsa, 83
Chile Cheese Crisp, 54
Chile Dusted Churros, 300–301, *301*
Chile Express, 125, *125*, 176, 181, 228, 289
Chile Filet Mignon, 208, 209
Chile Garlic Toast, 147, *147*
Chile Ham Breakfast Pie, 281
Chile-Infused Vodka, 30, *31*
Chile Lemon Drop Martini, 15, *15*
Chile Lemonitas, 2, *3*
Chile Mustard, 104

Glaze, 218; Simply Pickled Onions, 90; Spicy Sweet Tea, 4, *4*

lettuce: Crunchy Folded Tacos, 246–47; Hatch Chile Chicken Lettuce Wraps, 64, *65*; Hatch Cobb Salad, *130, 131*; Hatch Spicy Sub Sandwich, 200

lime: Frosty Chile Ritas, 20, *21*; Hatch Chile Ceviche, 61, *61*; Hatchelada, *12, 13*; Mexican Street Salad, 126, *127*; Sangrita, 14; Spicy Lime Spritzer, 5; Spicy Rocks Margarita, 19, *19*. *See also* Hatch Chile and Lime Mayo

Loaded Hatch Baked Potatoes, 142–43, *143*

Lobster Bisque Laced with Red Chile, 152–53, *153*

Lytle family, 228, *228*

Machaca Shredded Beef, 248–49

mango: Spicy Mango Margarita, 23

maple syrup: Hatch Caramel Maple Syrup, 286–87, *287*

margaritas: Frosty Chile Ritas, 20, *21*; Raspberry Chile Rita, 24, *25*; Spicy Mango Margarita, 23; Spicy Rocks Margarita, 19, *19*

marinara. *See* spaghetti sauce

marshmallow cream: Creamy Mexican Chocolate Fudge, 298–99, *299*

martinis: Chile Lemon Drop

Martini, 15, *15*; Hatch Chile Dirty Martini, 11

masa harina: Hatch Green Chile Tamales, 261–62

mayonnaise, 102, *102*; Hatch Chile Come Back Sauce, 106; Hatch Pimento Spread, 40; Hatch Potato Salad, 144. *See also* Hatch Chile and Lime Mayo

meatballs: Hatch Red Chile Meatball Bites, 72, *72*

meatloaf. *See* Hatch Chile Meatloaf

Mexican Chocolate Pecan Pie, 302

Mexican Mule, 28

Mexican Street Salad, 126, *127*

Migas and Pappas, 270

Mini Chile Corn Fritters, 74

Mini White Chocolate Raspberry Chile Shake, 8

mint: Hatch Whiskey Smash, 10; Spicy Lime Spritzer, 5; Spicy Sweet Tea, 4, *4*

Morrow Farms, 129, *129*, 206, *207*

muenster cheese: Chile Relleno Black Bean Bake, 234

mushrooms: Hatch Chile Chicken Lettuce Wraps, 64, *65*; Hatch Chile Stuffed Mushrooms, 58; Impossibly Good Chile Burger, 188–89

mustard: Chile Mustard, 104

nachos: Hatch Chile Nachos, 66

New Mexico Christmas-Style Burritos, 252, *253*

New Mexico Department of Agriculture, 149, 177, *177*, 179

New Mexico red chiles, 112–13, *113*, 117

New Mexico State University, Chile Pepper Institute at, xiii–xiv, 291

NuMex Big Jim, xvi

NuMex Heritage, xvi

NuMex Heritage Big Jim, xvii

NuMex R Naky, xvii

NuMex Sandia, xvi, 129, 228, 260

oil, dipping. *See* Hatch Chile Dipping Oil

olives: Hatch Chile Nachos, 66; Hatch Spicy Sub Sandwich, 200

onion: Chile and Caramelized Onion Flatbread, 204; Really Red Onion Relish, 88. *See also* Chile Spiced Caramelized Onions; Simply Pickled Onions

orange juice: Sangrita, 14

orange marmalade: Orange Chile Glaze, 94

pancake batter: Mini Chile Corn Fritters, 74

pancakes: Hotcakes with Hatch Maple Caramel Syrup, 286–87, *287*

Parmesan cheese: Crispy Hatch Chile Cheese Bites, 47; Green Chile Chicken Alfredo, 214, *215*; Green Chile Scones, 145; Hatch Chile

Village Market, xiv, 178, 181, 297, 297
vodka: Chile-Infused Vodka, 30, 31; Chile Lemon Drop Martini, 15, 15; Hatch Appletini, 22, 22; Hatch Chile Dirty Martini, 11; Hatch Nosh Bloody Mary, 16–17, 17; Pineapple Chile Shandy, 29

Whipped Blue Cheese and Chile Cream, 105
whiskey: Hatch Whiskey Smash, 10
white chocolate: Mini White Chocolate Raspberry Chile Shake, 8
White Spicy Sangria, 26, 27
wine, red: Red Chile Wine Sauce, 116
wine, white: Lobster Bisque Laced with Red Chile,

152–53, 153; Orange Chile Glaze, 94; White Spicy Sangria, 26, 27. *See also* Green Chile Wine Sauce
Witte, Jeff, 177, 177
wonton wrappers: Hatch Chile Wontons, 62
Worcestershire sauce: Hatch Nosh Bloody Mary, 16–17, 17; Sangrita, 14

yellow squash: Baked Squash and Chile, 132, 133; Spicy Veggie Salsa, 85
yogurt, 102, 102
Young Guns Hatch Chile Corporation, 18

zucchini: Baked Squash and Chile, 132, 133; Caldillo, 170, 171; Hatch Chile Spring Rolls, 48, 49; Spicy Veggie Salsa, 85

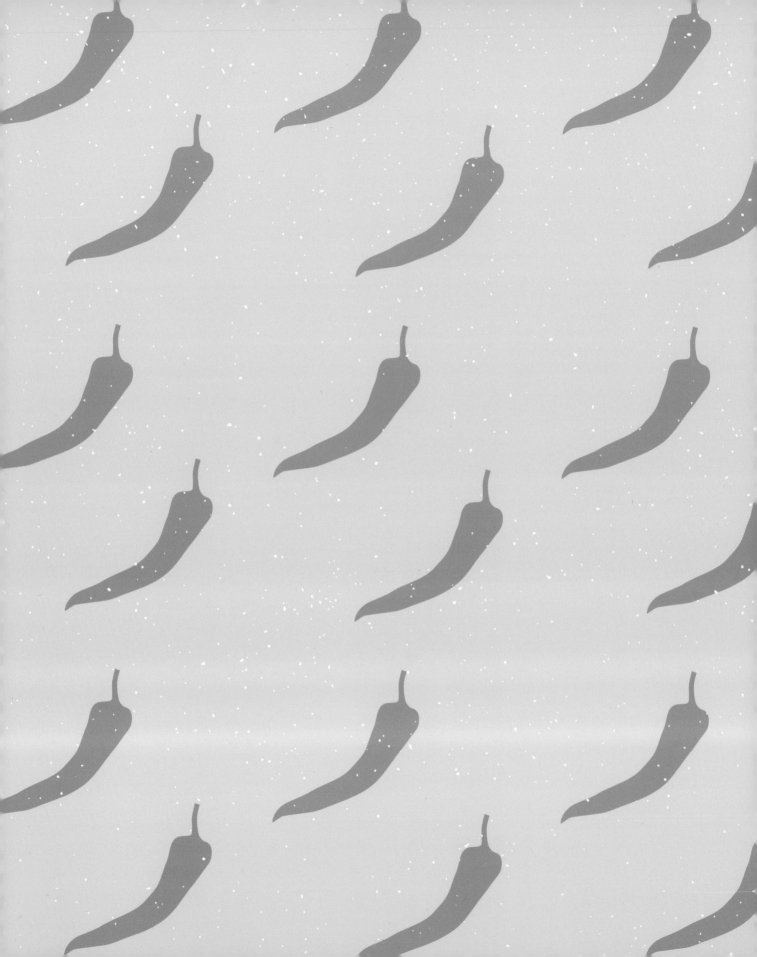